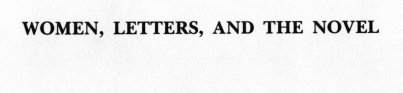

WOMEN, LETTERS, AND THE NOVEL

AMS Studies in the Eighteenth Century: No. 4

ISSN 0196-6561

Women,
Letters,
and the Novel

Ruth Perry

AMS PRESS, INC.
New York, N.Y.

Library of Congress Cataloging in Publication Data

Perry, Ruth, 1943-
    Women, letters, and the novel.

    (AMS Studies in the eighteenth century; no. 4)
    Bibliography: p.
    Includes index.
    1. English fiction—18th century—History and
criticism.   2. Epistolary fiction—History and
criticism.   3. Women and literature.   I. Title.
II. Series.
PR858.E65P4   823'.5'09352042   79-8637
ISBN 0-404-18025-6

MANUFACTURED
IN THE UNITED STATES OF AMERICA

To Curtis and Taylor

Table of Contents

Introduction

Novels have often been thought of as a woman's form, as the sentimental inheritors of the epics of men. For one thing, the interpersonal minutiae which replaced the action of battle were the traditional province of gossiping women rather than heroic warriors. For another, the lives so chronicled were often women's lives. When I began this study, I simply wanted to find out if there was any historical connection between women and the novel. I discovered that only a few women wrote novels during those early years of development and that more men than women bought these books during the years that they proliferated in booksellers' shops. However, there was another kind of connection to be made.

The changes in English society of the later seventeenth century and the early eighteenth century redefined the ways in which women were to function within that society, and at the same time prepared the context for the novel. Inasmuch as novels chart the private voyages of individual minds, these tracings were not a possible subject matter for popular fiction until the Reformation had emphasized the separate struggle and salvation of each single person; until the entrepreneurial spirit of capitalism had replaced community ties with sentimental attachment to individualism; until city living provided the anonymity which made private experience interesting to others; until people were reading and writing enough so that these private acts of consciousness were a substantial part of life for a sizable proportion of the population.

It is this emphasis on individual consciousness, on the mental motions which accompany action, that is the connection between novels and women. For novels developed at a time when literate women—the sort that figured in such books—were dispossessed of all meaningful activity save marrying and breeding, and when even these activities were to be done only in socially acceptable patterns. These genteel city women were the especial casualties of the capitalization of home industry and the separation of work places from dwelling places. They were specialized out of the economic life of the cities and settled into the separate, private, households which have always characterized urban life. In this changing society, novels embellished and perpetuated the myths of romantic love needed to strengthen the new economic imbalances between men and women and necessary to make the lives of the dispossessed seem fulfilled. Love-in-marriage was a sop that evolved for women as they lost their real power in the society.

Novels were the perfect vehicle for these fantasies of perfect happiness in an ideal love relation, for they worked in their readers' imagination blanking out the rooms in which they sat reading, and conjuring up other worlds for them to inhabit. In their very form they not only testified to the potency of life as it is imagined rather than as it is lived, but they also carried the cultural message that women's lives were to be spent in idleness, daydreams, and romance.

The irony is that such fictions, particularly those in letter form, were often passed off as historically true; that is, they were told according to the current conventions of realism and were passed off as anecdotes about living people. Because of the residual Puritan distaste for "falsehood," as well as the new craze for scientific objectivity, the contemporary preference for stories of "real people" dictated that much fiction be framed as first person writing: diaries, journals, travelogues, confessions, memoirs, autobiographies, and letters. The pretended realism of such love stories could only introduce expectations of romantic thrills and exciting amorous adventures to the isolated, bored, middle and upper-class women who were not part of the new expanding capitalism. Protected from the economic realities of life, they accepted their avocation for love in lieu of real work. Instead of being realistically assessed as contributing members of their society, they were idealized, set apart, robbed of their complex human identities, diminished to ornaments or to symbolic figures of moral purity.

This taste for first person writing, for personally verifiable documents, was probably also a symptom of the moral uncertainty of the period. The moral codes of previous generations existed as relics rather than as living principles, and people could no longer rely on those codes which connected their behavior to the culture's past. Since Descartes, it had been possible to conceive of truth as unhistorical, abstract, and individually determined. Without historical continuity in the moral realm, without the sense that an individual could use the guidelines evolved by earlier generations, each single case seemed important, each life story had some scraps of wisdom to help another. People compared notes, as it were, with the lives they found in books because there could be no standard except the actions of other men and women caught in the same historical situation.

Thus, epistolary fiction flourished in England long before Richardson wrote *Pamela*. Some of it was original, some translated from the French; some was burlesque, some didactic. The novels ranged in length from several hundred pages to brief stories told indirectly in one or two letters, buried in the pages of a weekly paper or in one of the many miscellaneous letter collections. Those which I will be calling epistolary novels were often less than seventy pages, sometimes bound several to the volume, costing between one and three shillings each. The plots often remind one of the plots of Restoration drama in which the characters outfox each other for sex, for money, or for marriage. But the stories are transformed in the new medium, arranged for private experience, for solitary reading at home, and there is a good deal more sentimental pulling of heart strings than rapid plot change or witty dialogue. For example, adultery is more apt to be an occasion for tragedy than for roguish humor in these fictions; and the subject is the painful progress of passion, rather than the triumphant manipulations of wit.

I have chosen the epistolary strain of the novel to study because letters were a very significant part of the written culture at that time, and because women seemed to have a special affinity for this personal one-to-one format. Also, stories told in letters are extremely literary to begin with because they are about people whose urge to communicate takes the form of writing. For a critic following the change from letters to fiction, from stories such as one tells about oneself to stories such as imagined characters might tell about themselves, there is the self-reflexive interest of fictions about fiction. These epistolary stories also foreshadow the purposes of novels as we know them, providing a coherent world to experience and permitting readers to live vicariously in the borrowed emotional lives of the characters. For the events in epistolary novels tend to be events of consciousness which take place on the pages of characters' letters rather than in any more active phase of their lives; by their very nature such novels are about subjective experience as synthesized for others. So quite incidentally to any sociological constructs about the development of the novel, a scrutiny of these early forms can tell one a good deal about the way fictions work. As the most direct predecessors of modern fiction, they first set out the formulas which novels in the tradition still follow.

This book begins with three chapters examining the London context of the developing novel, the peculiar and changed position of women in this world, and the dimensions of epistolary writing during this period. The next two chapters give a structural analysis of epistolary fiction in particular and suggest something about the mechanics of novels in general. The final chapter is an attempt to draw all this together: to show how novels developed in the ways they did in response to a particular historical situation which was redefining the family and changing the status of women. It connects the existence of this new class of women for whom the life of the imagination was more important than lived experience, with the development of the novelistic form which emphasizes the mental life of its characters. It is awkward to weave together historical facts and literary theory, but it is worth trying to do; otherwise theory becomes a pedantic exercise, and history remains barren and closed to the imagination.

Cambridge, Massachusetts, 1978

ACKNOWLEDGMENTS

I wish to thank John Hummel, in whose class the conception for this book began; Thomas A. Vogler, who directed the initial study with great intelligence and kindness; P. W. Shaw, who corresponded with me daily for two years while I considered epistolary relationships; Barbara Sirota and Janet Murray, who read the manuscript in its early stages; and Taylor Stoehr, whose presence has steadied and strengthened me.

I am grateful, too, to Ann Rourke and her staff for their indefatigable support, and to the librarians of the British Museum and Harvard's Houghton and Kress libraries for their patient assistance. An Old Dominion fellowship from the Massachusetts Institute of Technology made it possible for me to complete this study.

Jean Raoux (1677-1734). Young Woman Reading a Letter.
(The Louvre, Paris.)

1

Letter Fiction and the Search for Human Nature

London was a brutal and disorderly place in the late seventeenth and early eighteenth centuries. Ruffians lurked in the dirty, badly lit streets to rob and harass the wealthier citizens. John Evelyn was robbed several times at home and on the road. Samuel Pepys reports lying afraid in his bed at night, sure that the sounds he was hearing were thieves breaking into his house to steal his beloved possessions. Although the laws against theft were extreme—stealing a kerchief could be punished by death[1]—there continued to be a sizable criminal sub-culture of the sort described by Defoe in *Moll Flanders*.

In 1705 London's Common Council appointed more watchmen to keep peace in public streets; this action did not have its desired effect, though, for five years later it was reported that

> of late many loose, idle, and disorderly Persons have used in the Evenings, in a riotous and tumultuous Manner, to gather together in the Streets and other Passages of this city, and the Suburbs thereof; where they make Bonfires and Illuminations, stop the Coaches and assault the Persons of the Inhabitants, and other her Majesty's subjects who happen to pass by on their lawful Occasions, insult their Houses, break their Windows, forcibly and illegally demand Money of them. . . .[2]

In 1718 the City Marshall reported

> the general complaint of the taverns, the coffee-houses, the shop-
> keepers and others that their customers are afraid when it is dark to
> come to their houses and shops for fear that their hats and wigs
> should be snitched from their heads or their swords taken from
> their sides, or that they may be blinded, knocked down, cut or
> stabbed; Nay, the coaches cannot secure them, but they are
> likewise cut and robbed in the public streets, etc.[3]

Some of this crime was malicious, willful, unmotivated by
material need. There were, for instance, a band of local
hoodlums,

> who call themselves Hawkubites, and their mischievous invention
> of the work is, that they take people between hawk and buzzard,
> that is, between two of them, and making them turn from one to
> the other, abuse them with blows and scoffings; and if they
> pretend to speak for themselves, they then slit their noses, or cut
> them down the back.[4]

There were also a growing number of prostitutes, supplied
by the influx of country girls who came to London, helpless
and unsuspecting as one depicted in Hogarth's *The
Harlot's Progress*, unable to survive the disruptions of
enclosure and industrialization in their native towns, and
seeking employment as servants in the growing city.[5] The
many remedies for venereal disease advertised in the
London newspapers in the 1720s is probably a good index
of their increased activity.[6] And along the road leading out
of London lay an appalling number of abandoned children,
both dead and alive.[7]

In fact, living conditions in London in 1700 were so bad
that the death rate (one in twenty-five) far exceeded the
birth rate, a fact which alarmed a number of natural
philosophers who wrote about the necessity for marriage
and having more children.[8] This extraordinarily high waste
of life in the city occurred because of too much poisonous
gin (more stringent liquor licensing laws were not passed
until 1751), unsanitary quarters, bad food, disease, etc.

Throughout the eighteenth century the population of London had to be continually replenished by people pouring in from other towns and from the countryside.[9]

The rising numbers of marginal individuals without community or respectable work, and the squalor into which the city absorbed them, were signs of a society moving from an agricultural economy toward an industrial one. In many ways, the intellectual and philosophical changes in the culture were reflections of this critical economic shift. The old authorities were gone: the seventeenth century witnessed both the execution of the legitimate king and widespread religious dissent from traditional theology; nor had these orthodox sources of truth yet been repaired or replaced. It was an era in which abundant satire testified to the moral confusion, to the hypocritical gaps between pretended and actual standards. The culture paid lip service to the comfortable philosophy of the "great chain of being," in which individuals were required to blindly live out their parts in a Divine Plan so complicated that no one but God could understand its entire and perfect justice. Yet this philosophy was at odds with the newer spirit of entrepreneurial individualism which accompanied expanding trade and capitalism.

The literature is full of these contradictory signals. Robinson Crusoe, Pamela Andrews, Clarissa Harlowe, Tom Jones, all begin their adventures by leaving home, going off on their own, but each suffers for that willfulness and each is made to see the impossibility, in a social world, of doing exactly as one pleases. In each case, however, their enterprising spirit is rewarded as each achieves a higher station in life than that in which he or she began. This pattern is perhaps clearest in *Robinson Crusoe* where the sin committed by the hero—self-determination—is punishable by twenty-odd years of solitude and then rewarded with wealth.

Many of the criminal biographies, so popular in the early part of the eighteenth century, were shaped the same way, making it clear that each scoundrel's first important mis-step had been "individualism," ignoring Providence, and believing too exclusively in himself. Certainly this was the cause of Moll Flanders' unhappiness as well as of her success, and Defoe shows his readers at the end of that book that the only way to win personal salvation and public acclaim was to submit to the laws of God and of society. Similarly, the later parts of *Pamela* and of *Robinson Crusoe* are about the reclaiming of the individual by society: Pamela must learn to be the mistress of a bourgeois establishment, to fit into society at her new station, and Robinson Crusoe must cope with his sailors and the colony established on his once isolated and peaceful island. The attempt was to strike a new balance, to redefine the relation between needs of individuals and the rules of the larger society.

In the midst of these confusions, without clear ethical standards for living or unalterable social and economic places in which to fit, there was a growing belief that reason, aided by facts collected empirically, could supply the answers no longer provided by traditional religion or a divine-right monarchy. It was believed possible to under-stand human nature and prescribe rules for a healthy life through study and analysis rather than through revelation. After all, the seventeenth century had seen the discovery of the laws governing the universe; now it was time to do the same for humankind. As Ernst Cassirer observes:

> The whole eighteenth century is permeated by this conviction, namely, that in the history of humanity the time had now arrived to deprive nature of its carefully guarded secret, to leave it no longer in the dark to be marveled at as an incomprehensible mystery but to bring it under the bright light of reason and analyze it with all its fundamental force.[10]

The Royal Society, operating since 1660 with its studies of mathematics, astronomy, chemistry, and the natural sciences, was the institutional manifestation of the faith in the new methods of pursuing knowledge. Swift's materials for the satire of the experimenting mania in book III of *Gulliver's Travels* were not invented by him but came from the pages of *Philosophical Transactions*. Robert Boyle, for example, (who first enunciated the law that the volume of a gas varies inversely with pressure) was one of those who supplied him with instances in which the drive to corroborate scientific constructs with systematically gathered information exceeded the bounds of common sense. When Boyle described a blind Dutchman who could distinguish color by touch, "his most exquisite perception is in his thumb," and described his data with as much precision as in his more plausible experiments, Swift transformed the report into the blind man in Lagado who mixed colors for painters.[11]

Nor was curiosity the exclusive quality of a specialized group of academics. There was, at that time, a thirst for information among all those with the leisure and means to pursue it. The educated Englishman characteristically wanted to know more about the world in which he lived and about the people who inhabited it. A Frenchman visiting London in the early part of the century was struck by how universal was the English appetite for information and wrote home about it in this way:

> There are many shabby cafes in London with furniture which is worn because of the numbers of people frequenting them . . . What attracts the people to the cafes are the gazettes and other public papers. The English are great newsmongers. Most workers begin their day by going to a cafe to read the news. I have often seen bootblacks and others of that sort getting together to buy each day's gazette for a half-farthing and to read it together . . . There are a dozen different gazettes in London, some which come out every day, some twice a week and some weekly. One can read the news from other countries usually taken from the *Holland Gazette*. The articles on London are always the longest, one can learn of the marriage and death of people of quality, of civil, military and clerical appointments, and anything else of interest, comic and tragic, in this great city.[12]

The tastes of an increasingly literate public were beginning to determine what was printed in England, unlike in earlier times when writing was an aristocratic pursuit for a very select audience. Writers had to convince booksellers that their works could sell widely; it was no longer a matter of simply pleasing an aristocracy. Visual art, too, was moving toward public subscription rather than the patronage system with the establishment of the first academy of painting in 1711.[13] Newspapers were one of the visible signs of the demands of this new, broader audience. Indeed, modern notions of journalism—of simple, factual, objective, informative reporting—can be traced to this period. The lapsing of the Licensing Act in 1695 which had been a curb to publishing also encouraged the proliferation of this cheap reading matter. Coffee houses attracted customers by supplying newspapers to their clientele along with the latest beverages from the New World.

The popular demand for informative reading is also recognizable in the longer literary forms which sold well during the early part of the century. There were tales of travel, secret and not so secret histories of lives, and collections of letters. Certain terms recurred again and again in the titles of fiction: "history," "memoirs," "life," "voyage," "adventure," "account," "letters."[14] All of these forms were supposedly derived from materials which were authentic rather than fictional, for the public seemed to want to be informed about all the strange and marvelous permutations possible in real life.

The travel books were partly the result of the growth of capitalism: the impulse to accrue and the necessity for finding new business sent Englishmen all the way around the world, to return to talk of new lands and foreign people. As early as 1680 The Royal Society had shown an official interest in the accounts of travelers[15] and Evelyn's diary of August 6, 1698 reports the excitement of dining "at Mr. Pepys, where was Cap: Dampier, who had been a famous Buccaneere, brought hither the painted Prince Jolo, printed a Relation of his very strange adventures," discussing the errors in existing maps of the South Pacific.[16] Of course by 1720, this interest in the exotic South Pacific had grown sufficiently to blow up the famous South Sea bubble.

The letter, as form, was a perfect frame for travel reports or essays of any length and on any subject in this new age which so valued collecting information. (Indeed, the earliest newspapers were no more than batches of informative letters published together.)[17] Tone could range from impersonal journalistic human interest stories, to pedantic ethnographies, to ponderous theological debates, to sensational disclosures. Edward Ward, for example, was a hack writer who liked to masquerade his sensational exposés as on-the-scene reports back home in the form of letters.[18] While some had recourse to letters to debate the tenets of Quakerism or to detail foreign cultures, popular writers like Ward framed anything that might sell in a letter format.

Travel books were so popular by that time that after theology books they were the second most numerous kind of book published. But stories of voyages are also metaphoric expressions of testing limits. They are quite literally about how far one can go, pushing at boundaries, reducing unknowns to knowns. The travel literature which provided the public with anthropological lore about other civilizations often compared them to English society with an eye to finding out what was considered natural in other cultures, what customs corroborated one's own certainties about human limitations. Other environments were especially interesting for what they could show individuals about their own world. English courtship and marriage customs, in particular, were often compared to other cultures as if these differences could teach one how all of it ought to be done. Travel stories were also suitable as allegories of the favorite Puritan sort about losing and then finding one's way—wrestling with one's rebellious mind, straying into psychically alien territory, but finally turning homeward to the proper English way of life.

Pirate tales and criminal biographies, also very popular in the early part of the century, helped define good and evil in ways it would be hard to duplicate, with their examples of gratuitous and unreasoning violence at the extremes of human cruelty.[19] Indeed, the very interest in criminality presupposes an allegiance to law and order; it assumes that there is some basic standard from which deviations are made. There was an interest in unlawfulness for the same reasons that there was an interest in making up rules for living. Because man was still the most uncontrollable and unpredictable element in his own world, there was a need to examine the outer edges of human experience, in order to define the natural limits of the passions. So although the success of the criminal biographies can be explained by popular craving for the lurid and sensational, it could also be argued that these biographies satisfied a taste for the details about those who ended on the gallows, a curiosity as to how their lives led in that direction, what their experience consisted of, and how they came to be what they were. In fact, these accounts often did come from the records kept and published by the institutions processing these criminals, from reports of the trials at Old Bailey, and from published accounts which Newgate prison chaplains wrote about the last hours and confessions of criminals they had worked with. These chaplains sold their accounts for money and for the glory they earned with stories of their spiritual prowess in last minute conversions.[20]

It was an age of sermons, laws, rules, and fictionalized explorations of conduct and consequences, an age that believed reason could educate feeling. Therefore a market existed for books of advice on how to behave in even the most intimate moments of one's life. Popular writers of the day were certainly aware of that audience: John Dunton's *The Athenian Spy* (1704) was ready "to direct the Bachelor and the Virgin in their whole amour"[21] and Edward Ward's *Marriage Dialogues* (1708) meant to show those "unhappy in the Marry'd State" "where the fault lies." Defoe, always

willing to supply the needs of the reading public, contributed *The Family Instructor* (1715), a collection of sample
dialogues for sticky situations which might occur between
a father and son, or a mother and daughter—a "how-to-do-
it" manual for family life—and *Conjugal Lewdness* (1727)
which warns married couples at great length against too
heavy an emphasis on the sexual side of their union. It
should be remembered, too, that Richardson's letter-
writing manual offered directives to its readers for a good
deal more than style. It would seem that many readers
were looking for instruction in how to think and feel.

The many tales of love affairs bought eagerly by the
public at this time often featured a moralizing editorial
statement between the episodes of passion, dwelling on
the degree to which emotion could obliterate conscience
and pervert social relationships. Love always broke all the
rules, and created lawless behavior. As one novelist put it,

> Reason, Religion, and even the Will is subservient to that all-
> powerful Passion which forces us sometimes to Actions our Natures
> most detest; Mother against Daughter, Father against Son, con-
> trives; all Obligations of Blood and Interest are no more remem-
> ber'd; over every Bound we leap, to gratify the wild Desire, and
> Conscience but vainly interposes its Remonstrances.[22]

Perhaps there was a delicious horror in reading about such
"wild Desire" for the issue of what "our Natures most
detest" or the "Obligations of Blood and Interest" were not
easily defined. Stories of anarchic emotion teased the
imagination with the real range of human choices. Excessive desire, difficult to control and predict at best, could
push a person beyond self-control. Thus an early marriage
manual advises against incest "lest the Friendship a Man
bears to such a woman be immoderate; for . . . if the conjugal Affection be full and betwixt them as it ought to be,
and that it be over and above surcharged with that kindred
too, there is no doubt but such an Addition will carry the
Husband beyond the Bounds of Reason."[23] Love could lead

to madness; indeed it was seen as a kind of temporary insanity in which "Rape, Murder, everything that is shocking to Nature, and Humanity had in them Ideas less terrible than what despairing love presented . . ."24 Thus such tales demonstrated what social philosophers believed at that time—that people were held in check only by the laws and customs which regulated individual passions, that they were creatures of appetite whose instincts headed them toward chaos but for the restraints of reason.

Sometimes these love stories were offered up in a spirit of scientific humanism, as case studies in emotion. Like the criminal biographies they offered a close up view of the uncivilized side of human nature. This rationale was all the more convincing as the conventions which defined fiction became increasingly realistic; for as one popular writer pointed out, moral prescriptions based on fictional lives are more likely heeded when "fear of falling into the like Misfortunes, causes us to interest ourselves more in their Adventures, because that those sorts of Accidents may happen to all the World; and it touches so much the more because they are the common Effects of Nature."25 The public wanted more of the sense that such stories were based on "real life" and that one could learn from individual cases. In 1705 Mrs. Manley announced this literary trend: the fad for French romances was "very much abated" and "Little Histories" had taken their place.26 In 1719 Defoe assured his readers that "a private Man's Adventures in the World were worth making Publick."

Some of the "Little Histories" of that time strain the modern sense of realism considerably. Take, for example, this letter from a servant girl asking advice of an all-knowing seer about her affair with her master:

> I believe, indeed, he has a great Respect for me, for he always takes care to cut the best bit of the Meat, or Fowl, or whatever we have for our Dinner, and lay it on his Plate as if he design'd to eat it himself, and leaves it for me.27

This detail, touching in its homeliness, is meant to testify to the everyday reality of the tale and to give the reader some insight into the experience of the character. Yet in its own way, it is as naively romantic as a story of a damsel saved from distress.

Nevertheless, the effect of writing vignettes about probable characters rather than allegorical sequences or fantastic adventures, of focusing on concrete physical details rather than falling back on indistinct, stylized descriptions, of shortening length and deflating style, was to blur distinctions between fantasy and mundane reality and make it seem possible to move romance into the realm of daily life. The outlandish and fanciful names of characters in the romances began to be used as the pseudonyms in epistolary fiction, assumed by clandestine correspondents to avoid detection in case their letters were intercepted. It also was becoming literary fashion to write about middle-class heroes and heroines, a practice which the very prolific Eliza Haywood defended in this way:

> Those who undertake to write Romances, are always careful to give a high Extraction to their *Heroes* and *Heroines*; because it is certain we are apt to take a greater Interest in the Destiny of a *Prince* than of a *private Person*. We frequently find, however, among those of a middle State, some, who have Souls as elevated, and Sentiments equally noble with those of the most illustrious Birth: Nor do I see any Reason to the contrary; *Nature* confines not her Blessings to the *Great* alone ... As the following Sheets, therefore, contain only real Matters of Fact, and have, indeed, something so very surprising in themselves, that they stand not in need of any Embellishments from Fiction: I shall take my *Heroine* such as I find her, and believe the Reader will easily pass by the Meanness of her Birth, in favour of a thousand other good Qualities she was possess'd of.[28]

In arguing that human qualities which are worth emulating can be found throughout the population, she at once announces that her book has a moral function and heightens the impression that her characters come from life, that her stories "contain only real Matters of Fact" and "stand not in need of any Embellishments from Fiction." Nor is this example unique. A passage from the translation of Marivaux' *The Life of Marianne* (1736) strikes the same notes: there is an inverse snobbishness aimed at those who do not like to read about ordinary people and an implication that the story of a tradesman or commoner is as valuable a "History of the human Heart" as anyone could wish, and probably truer:

> There are People whose Vanity creeps into every Thing they do, even into their very Reading. Lay before them the History of the human Heart, among People of great Quality; no Doubt they will think it an important Matter, and well worth their Attention ... No Matter for all the rest of Mankind. They barely allow them to live, but judge them with no further Notice. They would even insinuate, that Nature might very well have spared the Production of such Creatures, and that Tradesmen and Commoners are but a Dishonour to her. You may judge then with what Scorn such Readers as these would have looked upon me.[29]

The day of the poor but honest heroine had arrived, thanks to the demands of a less aristocratic reading public who wanted to read more stories about people from their own class staunchly upholding strict moral codes.

The audience for whom these early novels were written were generally Londoners with enough education and leisure to read, and enough money to buy the books. Since they cost six pence to six shillings at that time (one or two shillings being the common price), they were out of range of all but the well-to-do. Epistolary fiction, sometimes printed piecemeal in magazines, was a little cheaper, installments running only six to twelve pence a week that way.[30] The effect of watching the story unfold, of waiting for the next installment, was particularly well suited to the form of a novel told in letters. But whether serially or by volume, reading novels was a taste that only the comfortable classes could indulge. Private entertainment is expensive, and reading one's own book cost a good deal more than communal theater-going which had been the literary amusement of an earlier generation. Still, books were selling better than ever before, and the increased volume of sales kept their price stable in spite of a steady rise in the cost of printing.[31]

Although these books were fairly expensive, the main audience for them was not aristocratic. For one thing, the villainous rakes most often cast as the enemy in these stories came from that class, and the satire tends towards mockery of class distinctions from a middle-class point of view. For example, in Mrs. Davys' *Familiar Letters Betwixt a Gentleman and a Lady*, there is a butler whose proof of being "a very well-bred Man" is that he "drinks, whores, and games and has just as much Estate as will qualify him for a vote," as well as an impoverished peer who has gambled away his estate and whose hovel is satirically called "my Lord's chamber."[32] The focus on the heroines in these novels also betrays a particularly middle-class concern, for it was the only class in which men worked and women did not. (Among the laboring classes men and women both worked; aristocratic men and women had similar requirements in the way of duties.) This divergence of role led to great controversy about the nature of their relationship to one another. Then, too, the growing need in landed aristocratic families for middle-class cash made middle-class women upwardly mobile as they had never been before. This intensified the middle-class interest in themes of love, marriage, and the etiquette of sexual fencing.

The letter novel thrived in this context. Middle-class readers could identify with characters who sat down to write letters which told of the agonies of love, or reported experiences of traveling, or revealed secrets, or gave advice, or arranged intrigues. They could read about the thoughts and experiences of these literate heroes and heroines with the appealing illusion that they came directly from the minds of the participants rather than being filtered through the sensibility of an omniscient narrator. The language generally used in epistolary fiction was common rather than literary, and the characters who wrote news to their families or advice to their friends were all plausible types. The letters themselves seemed to be proof that such people really existed and that following their lives was not merely self-indulgent escape, but informative reading about first-hand experience.

Certainly the most interesting experiments in realistic fiction of the day were books written like autobiography— *Moll Flanders* or *Robinson Crusoe* or letter novels. The public must have enjoyed such first-hand writing, for columns of letters of complaints, advice, or confession written to editors of newspapers and gazettes by private individuals were so successful that editors imitated them, and featured professionally written ones concocted to read like unsolicited letters. It was simply easier to commission them than to collect them, and the public was always curious about others like themselves, isolated in their separate lives within the big city.

Because letters were the obvious medium for exchanging informal and personal news between intimates, they also perfectly illustrated stories of relationships. The epistolary mode gave an objective cast to such stories, as if they were data collected from actual experience demonstrating the natural extremes of feeling and depicting human problems. Even the titles of epistolary novels sometimes seem to·lay claim to special truth about human states like curiosity or love or constancy or jealousy or innocence, as if the letters made it possible to abstract and isolate them for special study in each story: "The Masqueraders, or *Fatal Curiosity*," "Fantomina, or *Love in a Maze*," "The Fatal Secret or *Constancy in Distress*," "The Penitant Hermit or *The Fruits of Jealousy*," "The Player's Tragedy or *Fatal Love*," "The Brothers or *Treachery Punish'd*" (italics mine).

This kind of epistolary writing tended to be very much in

demand in the forty years or so which preceded Richardson's *Pamela*, perhaps because it satisfied the public taste
for "realism" or seemed to provide documentation for
moral dilemmas, and because it was written not as literary
art but to sell to the middle class readers whose values and
interests it reflected. In any case there were between
100 and 200 epistolary works published and sold in
London during the early eighteenth century, many of them
very popular, running through many editions. Some of
them were collections of separate, unconnected letters,
each of which was exemplary, amusing, or informative;
some were novels constructed entirely with letters; some
were intermediate cases—collections of "real life" letters
which were sequential but did not quite tell a story, or
novels with interpolated letters but with plots much too
complicated to be narrated through the indirection of
letters. This cluster of letter fiction provides the seeding
for the subsequent development of English novels; close
inspection of the form in later chapters will show how the
letter format encouraged certain tendencies in fiction,
made it possible for women to do such writing professionally, and because of the inevitable assumptions and themes
of stories told in letters, made fashionable the tales of
endless maneuvering between men and women.

All of the best selling Grub Street hack writers dealt in
letters: Defoe, Dunton, Ward, Brown, D'Urfey, and by the
1720s, Eliza Haywood and Mary Manley as well. They
translated them, edited them, "presented" them or wrote
them outright; many letters were passed off as authentic,
some were facetious, some were fictional. Eliza Haywood
alone issued eighteen volumes of epistolary work between
1724 and 1727 which means that there was a great demand
for them, for her livelihood depended on writing what
would sell. Edmund Curll, the most famous, successful,
and unscrupulous bookseller of this period was making
most of his money by 1719 on letter collections and fictive
autobiographies.[33] This was the same bookseller called

"unspeakable" by Pope in his denunciation of the whole
new upstart literary industry which was upsetting the
tradition of literature as an aristocratic occupation. A later
critic of the period wrote more kindly of Curll's propensity
to print private papers as his "indefatigable industry in
preserving our national remains."[34]

But not only did the middle class profit from the opening
up of the literary profession. Educated women, too, now
found it possible to make a living writing stories according
to the popular formula, or publishing diaries or letters in a
culture which thought it anomalous for a gentlewoman to
produce anything more public. Women's writing, of course,
was not taken seriously but thought of as a new, pleasant
way for women to busy themselves. A reader wrote to *The
Spectator,*

> You lately recommended to your Female Readers, the good old
> custom of their Grandmothers, who used to lay out a great Part of
> their Time in Needle-work: I entirely agree with you in your
> Sentiments, . . . I would, however, humbly offer to your Consider-
> ation the Case of the Poetical Ladies; who, though they may be
> willing to take any Advice given them by the *Spectator,* yet can't
> so easily quit their Pen and Ink, as you may imagine.[35]

The Preface to Lady Mary Wortley Montagu's *Turkish
Letters,* written in 1724 by the first English feminist, Mary
Astell, was unusual in its warm praise of the female
sensibility. Mary Astell, who had long decried women's
servitude, pressing for women's right to a real education,
asked her audience to set aside their prejudices against
women's writing and be "pleased that a *woman* triumphs,
and proud to follow in her train."[36] The woman she cham-
pioned, Lady Mary Wortley Montagu, was one of the few
women in the intellectual circles of the day. She was a
gifted writer and an astute conversationalist, at one time
very much admired by Pope, although later estranged from
him. Mary Astell claimed that her letters from Turkey were

proof that ladies traveled "to better purpose" than their lords, and that while the public was "surfeited with *Male Travels*, all in the same tone, and stuft with the same trifles; a lady has the skill to strike out a new path, and to embellish a worn-out subject, with a variety of fresh and elegant entertainment."[37] Certainly Lady Mary traveled "to better purpose" than even elegant entertainment, for it was she who brought back to England the practice of innoculation against small-pox.

Indeed, there were a number of successful woman novelists in the decades preceding the publication of Richardson's *Pamela*, in spite of the fashionable derision of "Literary Ladies." Interestingly, all of them—Behn, Manley, Davys, Haywood, Rowe—wrote at least some of their fiction in the form of letters. One of the reasons women were encouraged to try their hands at epistolary fiction was because it was a format that required no formal education. It did not treat traditional literary problems, it necessitated no scholarly training. Its success largely depended on a simple, personal, letter-writing style. This was, in fact, one of the few kinds of writing which had long been encouraged in women since—to make the appropriate distinction—letter-writing had always been thought of as an accomplishment rather than as an art.

But it is important to remember that women did not dominate this new sort of fiction although they wrote a good deal of it. The most authoritative checklist of pre-Richardson epistolary fiction includes seventy-two volumes written by men and fifty-four volumes written by women, of which Eliza Haywood alone wrote twenty-nine.[38] It is possible, of course, that women contributed more to epistolary fiction than we can ever know, for sixty-eight of those 200 or so early epistolary works[39] have no known authors and it is often thought that respectable women took refuge behind the label "anonymous."

At the same time that women began to write professionally, they also became a significant new audience for the fiction and light reading coming from the new Grub Street industry. Certainly the proportion of women readers in the audience had been much less half a century earlier. A study of 262 works printed in a ten-year span in the middle of the seventeenth century shows that although twenty-nine were dedicated to specific women, only nine of the books were explicitly intended for a female readership.[40] Nor had women been the main audience for the romances of the seventeenth century. William Temple recommended several long romances to Dorothy Osborne in the course of their courtship; Samuel Pepys read romances and even tried his amateur's hand at writing one. On January 30, 1664 his diary entry reads:

> This evening, being in the humour of making all things even and clear in the world, I tore some old papers; among others, a romance which (under the title of 'Love a Cheate') I begun ten years ago at Cambridge; and at this time reading it over tonight I liked it very well. . . .

But by the beginning of the eighteenth century, a sizable female audience was beginning to be assumed for fiction of all sorts. The preface to Mme. D'Aulnoy's *The Present Court of Spain* calls attention to its female writer because it "will go a great way you know with the Ladies and admirers of Ladies. . . ."[41] Edward Ward's *Female Policy Detected: or The Arts of a Designing Woman Laid Open* (1695) was certainly written because of the growing market for books about women. Dunton, never one to miss a good commercial opportunity, advertised a book of "600 letters pro and con, on all the Disputable Points relating to Women" called *The Female Warr*. It is interesting that he thought the letter the most believable way of presenting women's voices. Steele, too, considered his treatment of women's topics in *The Spectator* as new and daring since no other magazine had ever set out to "treat on Matters which relate to Females, as they are concern'd to approach, or fly from the other Sex, or as they are tyed to them by

Blood, Interest, or Affection."[42] The novelty of his venture
is partly visible in the uncertain tone with which he treats
women's issues. On the one hand he professed an interest
in elevating them to a shared intellectualism with men,
deploring the lack of opportunities for women's education
and recognizing the harmful effects of the differential
attitudes of parents towards their girl and boy children. On
the other hand, he patronized, with amusement, the diminished world which women inhabited:

> I have often thought there has not been sufficient Pains taken in
> finding out proper Employments and Diversions for the Fair ones.
> Their Amusements seem contrived for them rather as they are
> Women than as they are reasonable Creatures; and are more
> adapted to the Sex than to the Species. The Toilet is their great
> Scene of Business, and the right adjusting of their Hair the
> principal Employment of their Lives ... Their most Serious
> Occupations are Sowing and Embroidery, and their greatest
> Drudgery the Preparation of Jellies and Sweet-meats.[43]

The new audience for the incidental prose of letter
collections, magazines, and epistolary fiction in the early
eighteenth century also continued to include many men.
Dudley Ryder for instance, a pleasant middle-class young
man whose diary survives, was an avid reader both of letter
collections and of essays from *The Spectator* and *The
Tatler* for their sensible "reflections and observations upon
the passions, tempers, follies and vices of mankind."[44] One
hundred and eighty-six of the 309 names of people engaged to buy a copy of *Letters From a Lady of Quality to a
Chevalier* (costing three to five shillings depending on the
binding) are men's names;[45] seventy-four percent of the
names on the subscription list bound with the 1730 edition
of *Some Memoirs of the Amours and Intrigues of a Certain
Irish Dean* are men's names; 198 out of 332 subscribers for
Elizabeth Boyd's *The Happy Unfortunate or The Female
Page* (costing two shillings six pence in advance and an
equal sum upon delivery) are men; in five out of six of the

subscription lists for epistolary novels reported on by
Robert Day, men subscribers outnumber women subscribers two to one.[46] It would seem that in spite of the
increasing number of women's voices and women's issues
reaching the public, men were still the main purchasers of
literature in that period. Part of the explanation for this, no
doubt, is that men tended to control the money in a family.
Furthermore, booksellers' shops, like coffee houses, were
still men's territory, unusual places for a gentlewoman to
be found.

Considering that men still dominated the world of popular literature it is remarkable how many of the central
characters in these novels are women. The stories are
created so that the reader watches their dilemmas, which
are usually sexual, unfold. In the older chivalric romances
it had always been a man's honor which was tested, not a
woman's—and that honor had altogether different properties from those at issue in the eighteenth-century novel. In
the tradition of Adam and Eve, Samson and Delilah,
Aeneas and Dido, it had always been the woman who
seductively lured the man from his higher purpose, his
noble mission. When Sir Gawain in the Arthurian romance
Sir Gawain and the Green Knight allowed himself to be
seduced by a woman it was a punishable weakness in his
knightly character, a flaw in his single-minded per-
severance. In the literature of chivalry, a man's honor
resided in his physical prowess and his spiritual enlightenment which were his weapons against the forces of evil
often tempting him in the form of a sexually inviting
woman. By the time of Richardson, these roles had been
very much reversed, and without any sense of strain the
public read its way tearfully through 2,000 pages of an
unscrupulous rake trying to seduce a poor, defenseless
woman. As a social philosopher at the turn of the century
noted, "Men are now the Tempters, and *Women* . . . are
first *ashamed* of their *offense*."[47] No longer were men
expected to test their mettle by stoic endurance against

tremendous odds—dragons, sorcery, hostile bands of knights. No longer did a man display his "greedy hardiment" by eager combat with challengers. The contest had narrowed considerably by the end of the seventeenth century; a man's trophies were his sexual conquests, and it was the woman who fought the holy struggle to preserve her chastity.

In these fictions, a woman's chastity stood for a more profound inviolability, for being able to hold onto one's convictions and not buckle under pressure. It was her passive endurance, her ability to keep saying "no" in the face of increasingly extreme pressure that was being tested. An early epistolary story by Thomas Brown, for example, shows the connection between chastity and independence; for as long as the husband could not possess his wife sexually he could not "invade" her in any other way either. Only when "the Castle surrender'd" after two months, could the husband control her entirely.[48]

One feels certain that these sexual conflicts were about power rather than desire because the male sexuality is so aggressive. In Crébillon *fils'* novel *Letters from the Marchioness de M**** as in *Clarissa*, the woman actually dies of the sexual invasion. The military metaphors in *Captain Ayloffe's Letters* which are standard in the eighteenth-century language of love, are very much to the point; that is, the object of the game was winning as much as pleasure. "Women are like Commanders in small Garrisons," reads Captain Ayloffe's advice to his friend, "reject the *Carte Blanche*, and pretend to maintain the last Man; but when your Approaches are made, and the Batteries play smartly upon 'em, they'l hang out the Flag, and that Town is not far from Surrendring, which begins to Parley."[49] Or take this letter which a man writes to the woman he loves in *Love-Letters Between A Nobleman and His Sister*. He is telling her of a dream he has just had:

... it was then, and there me thought my *Sylvia* yielded, with a

faint Struggle and a soft Resistance; I heard her broken Sighs, her
tender whispering Voice, that trembling cry'd—Oh! Can you be so
cruel.—Have you the Heart—Will you undo a Maid because she
loves you? Oh! Will you ruin me because you may? My faithless—
My unkind—then sigh'd, and yielded, and made me happier than a
triumphing God! But this was still a Dream, I wak'd and sigh'd,
and found it vanish'd all![50]

He dreams about "triumphing," fighting and taking and
being deified, potent as a God! Like most of the seduction
struggles, this one too is really a power struggle.

One of the reasons for this sexual aggressiveness against
women in epistolary novels is because it is precisely the
impotent suffering of the embattled heroine which pro-
duces the anguished consciousness that needs the release
of writing letters. In these stories, women are imprisoned,
seduced, abducted, raped, abandoned, and their passively
outraged responses to these developments are carefully
detailed. Because the woman's role is stereotypically re-
active rather than active, the woman's side of things maxi-
mizes emotional self-examination. After each encounter,
each new plot development, the heroine is given no
recourse but to retire to the privacy of her writing closet
and react on paper.

Indeed, these epistolary novels are often plotted like
experiments performed on isolated individuals. The characters are almost systematically manipulated and their
reactions under pressure carefully preserved in their letters or journals. Both Pamela and Clarissa are put through
paces to see if they pass the test of virtue. Certainly in a
civilization steeped in the Christian tradition of wander-
ings in the wilderness and of finally finding salvation,
stories of trials are no novelty. Yet these references to tests
and trials are not so allegorical in tone as they are experi-
mental. One of Aphra Behn's women writes "I'll die before
I'll yield my Honour . . . if I can stand this Temptation, I
am Proof against all the World."[51] "If it had not been for
this Trial to get the Mastery of my Passion," states another

embattled heroine in another epistolary novel, "I should never have understood the force of it."[52] The books direct the reader's attention to the heroine's responses as she confronts difficulty after difficulty, to be recorded in her letters, as if the emotional particulars of each case are what is important rather than any temporary outcome in the plot.

Perhaps it was because women were so separated from the rest of society, so very much on their own psychologically, that they came to be the symbolic figures who battled for integrity in the new forms of fiction. Even if a woman conformed totally to the expectations her family held for her, she never was really established securely. Her position was so perennially marginal that one misstep could always lose her everything, and she usually had nothing but her own strength of will and character to pull her through. No one in the society was as alone as a woman; she had no personal power, no resources, and if cut off from her parents, no allies. This defenselessness is apparent enough in a Pamela or a Moll Flanders, but a married woman, too, out of favor with her husband, could be as isolated as described in *The Fatal Amour Between a Beautiful Lady and a Young Nobleman*: "She saw herself in the Hands of an angry Husband, who had an absolute Power over her: And had no body to advise or comfort her."[53] Often these fictional heroines are orphans, lonely individuals standing outside the culture who therefore can be the test cases for working out a new balance between society's regulation and individual desire.

When fictional heroines vacillated about leaving their parental homes and making their own choices, or when fictional rakes debated internally about indulging their desires or following the community's moral codes, they were reflecting dilemmas new to the culture. In part, these were caused by economic changes.[54] For example, the issue of whether to marry for reasons of estate or for individual preference was a very real question in England at that time. But other problems were metaphorically tested in tales of women's virtue and desire as well: whether or not there were natural moral limits, whether the claims of society and traditional authority ought to come before the needs and passions of an individual.

In the epistolary story by Aphra Behn called *Love-Letters Between A Nobleman and His Sister* (1694), these things come together clearly. It is about an incestuous and adulterous passion which is discussed for a long time in letters before finally being consummated near the end of the story. In his verbal agonies, the hero Philander often writes about what is natural and what is artificially imposed upon man by misguided social codes. He is made to be a spokesman for the more "natural," animal side of human nature, envying the freedom of wild birds who are not restrained by "troublesome Honour:"

> Man, the Lord of all! He to be stinted in the most valuable Joy of Life; Is it not pity? Here is no troublesome Honour, amongst the pretty Inhabitants of the Woods and Streams, fondly to give Laws to Nature, but uncontroul'd they play, and sing, and love; no Parents checking their dear Delights, no Slavish Matrimonial Ties to restrain their nobler Flame. No Spies to interrupt their blest Appointments. . . .[55]

He questions the social definitions of what is acceptable, and proclaims his right to "incestuous" love. Indeed, when one looks closely at the nobleman and his mistress-sister, Sylvia, it is clear that there are some extenuating circumstances. For one thing, Sylvia is not Philander's actual blood sister but his wife's younger sister, although that relationship still has an incestuous feel to it. For another, his wife is cuckolding *him* with someone else. But Sylvia argues "False as she is, you are still married to her."[56] Because the social codes are taken seriously, the novel is shaped by that struggle over morality.

The characters all realize that there are laws which feeling does not sweep away; throughout there are references to the affair as being "criminal," "monstrous." When they are discovered, Sylvia writes to her lover:

> *Philander*, all that I dreaded, all that I fear'd is fallen upon me: I have been arraign'd and convicted; three Judges, severe as the three infernal ones, sate in Condemnation on me, a Father, a Mother and a Sister. . . .[57]

Her love affair is an illegal one, and she sees in her family's condemnation the disapproval of the larger society. Sylvia's legalistic metaphor foreshadows the real legal action which follows, too, for the larger society does seek to punish the illicit lovers. Philander is pursued by lawsuits for rape and incest. Finally they solve their problem by marrying Sylvia off to one of Philander's lackeys, who agrees to be married in name only, acting as a front for Philander himself. The only way to appease the outraged society is to mimic its conventions, even in travesty.

Although the lovers hide from their parents, and try to outwit the conventions of society, there is no gaiety about this truancy. Throughout this book there is a deep fear of the breakdown of authority. Although Philander decries the social codes, at the same time the reader feels how much they are needed to hold together the society. Vague and shadowy, the execution of Charles I hovers in the background as a warning of where disrespect for law and order can lead. Philander is a political rebel as well as a sexual one; Sylvia denounces his secret revolutionary activities because they could lead to king-killing and sacrilege. She writes to Philander as if there were a mystical and religious sanction against questioning authority: "I am certain that should the most harden'd of your bloody Rebels look him in the Face," she says, referring to the king, "the devilish Instrument of Death would drop from his sacrilegious Hand, and leave him confounded at the Feet of the Royal forgiving Sufferer . . .[58] Certainly this passage is naive; but more than that, it is invested with great religious fervor suddenly and sharply felt. In fact, the energy seems to come from Sylvia's anxiety and displaced sexual intensity, expressed in these political issues. Her exaggerated reaction connects the breaking of the two kinds of rules.

This story of crime, both incest and treason, told in the love letters between Philander and Sylvia, looks much like the same old seduction story. Philander convinces Sylvia, against law and common sense, that their desire for one another is more important than anything else. But closer to the surface than usual, the concerns of a culture in flux can be seen, trying to mediate in its fiction between the claims of the traditional and the individual's questioning of these conventions.

Because the epistolary novel grew in response to certain specific social conditions—a new literary industry, broader literacy in the population, the evolution of the female audience, the development of a few writers among middle and upper class women—it was a form well suited to a detailed working through of moral issues. Characters who spent their fictional lives writing letters to each other about their confusion and ambivalence contributed to an illusion of realism; these emotional outpourings were the literary residue of deeply felt experience and thought from which a reader might learn something of use in order to deal with his own moral dilemmas.

2

The Economic Status
of Women

It is necessary to look closer at the economic situation of women at the end of the seventeenth century, to clarify the nature of the social changes which were altering English culture, and which were reflected in the fiction. For it was during this same historical period which gave rise to the novel that new family patterns were established and that many of the myths of love and sexuality which still hold sway first flourished. They developed with the rest of the apparatus of the modern age—with capitalized economy, division of labor, exclusive property relations of individual nuclear families, city living—in the seventeenth century, as women relinquished their traditional claims to work. The re-shuffling of the economic functions of men and women which accompanied England's movement into trade and manufacture goes a long way toward explaining the pre-occupation with love and marriage in the standard plots of epistolary novels.[1]

One way to begin this examination is to compare women's economic rights in the Middle Ages with women's economic rights at the beginning of the eighteenth century. In the Middle Ages, property rights entailed feudal services to an overlord, and while women often gave over the rights to work the land—and the responsibility for feudal services—to their husbands, their individual legal connection to the land was never bypassed. Women were also enfeoffed in their own right, and required to provide arms or perform customary services in exchange for their holdings.[2]

No medieval husband could dispose of his wife's property without her free consent. Nor was a woman's inheritance treated like a dowry; each could manage her own inherited holdings as would a single woman, obligated only to feudal lords. If a husband mismanaged his wife's property or deprived her of her due proceeds from it, she had legal means to protect herself. Women had separate legal rights from their husbands' to make petitions and testify in court: man and wife were not legally considered "one."[3]

Marriage was a religious and economic arrangement which did not necessarily demean the status of women. They shared the responsibilities of that arrangement with their husbands. When men were called to the crusades or the internecine battles among overlords, women managed the land and households in their absence. In fact, it has been thought that the origins of chivalry can be found in this situation. Vassals on the land swore their fealty and obedience to the wife of their feudal lord while he was off fulfilling *his* feudal obligations elsewhere.

Woman also did productive labor in medieval society. They were members of guilds to which they paid cash fees and dues, and they hired their own apprentices. Their daughters as well as their sons were eligible for membership in these guilds. Married or not, they were responsible for their own debts. Mary Beard reports that women were barbers, tailors, tylers, joiners, carpenters, furriers, saddlers, spurriers. Another economic historian, F. W. Tickner, points out that our language carries the record of these occupations of women. The suffix *ster* indicated a female worker. Thus because there are Websters today, we

know that women did weaving. Baxters were professional
bakers. Brewsters were brewers, and Spinsters were spinners.[4]
   By the early eighteenth century, this situation was very
much altered. There was little chance for economic self-
sufficiency for women of the middle class. Dorothy Osborne kept house for her father, but when he died she was
left without the right to any home. Moll Flanders' adventures illustrate how a single woman had to scramble for her
living in the early eighteenth century—and how marriage
was one of the very few legal occupations open to her. A
protest against this state of affairs can be found in the
Gentleman's Magazine of 1739 in which an anonymous
reader suggests that young women without dowries be
"put Apprentices to genteel and easy Trades, such as
Linnen or Wollen Drapers, Haberdashers of small Wares,
Mercers, Glovers, Perfumers, Grocers, Confectioners,
Retailers of Gold and Silver Lace, Buttons, etc." And
indeed, it is remarkable that only two or three women's
names appear among several hundred linen-drapers, tailors, hosiers, druggists etc. on a list of guild subscribers to
W. Maitland's *History and Survey of London* (1739). This
contemporary social critic then goes on to ask the obvious
question.

"Why are not these as creditable Trades for the Daughters of
Gentlemen as they are for their Sons; and all of them more proper
for Women than Men? Is it not as agreeable and becoming for
Women to be employ'd in selling a Farthing's Worth of Needles, a
Halfpenny Lace, a Quarter Yard of Silk, Staff, or Cambrick, as it is
absurd and ridiculous to see a Parcel of young Fellows, dish'd out
in their Tie-Wigs and Ruffles, the Lords of the Creation, as Men
affect to be call'd, busied in Professions so much below the
Honour and Dignity of their Sex.

"There are few Trades in which women cannot weigh and measure as well as Men, and are so capable of selling as they, and I am
sure will buy as cheap, and perhaps cheaper: For they can go to the
wholesale Merchant's House, and purchase their Goods; whereas
the Men generally transact all Business of this kind in Taverns and

Coffee-houses, at a great additional Expence, and the loss of much time. . . .

"If Women were train'd up in Business from their early Years, 'tis highly probable they would in general be more industrious, and get more Money, than Men; and if so, what Woman of Spirit would submit to be a slave, and fling herself away, as many are forc'd to do, merely for a Maintenance, because she cannot stoop to be a servant, and can find no reputable Business to go into?"[5]

These were actually rather strong words for this time, and while they do not illustrate a typical sentiment, they do dramatize a very real problem of the period.

By the end of the seventeenth century, unmarried women in their fathers' homes, had the status of dependent children. The idea of pin money, the income which a husband gives his wife for her own spending, appears when this economic dependence is firmly fixed in the culture. Elizabeth Pepys, Samuel Pepys' wife, continually begged her husband for money until he finally settled a regular allowance on her. In 1697 the term *pin money* was new enough to be city slang: "These Londoners have a gibberidge with 'em would confound a Gipsy. That which they call pin-money is to buy their wives everything in the varsal world."[6] In *The Spectator* fifteen years later, Steele wrote that the notion of pin money "is of very late Date, unknown to our Great Grandmothers. . . ."[7]

All properties which a woman brought with her to a marriage, usually in the form of a dowry, automatically became her husband's at the time of the marriage. If he died first, he could not "will" her property away, but while he lived the properties were legally his. A woman could make no contract or other legal arrangement without a husband's consent. She could neither sell, pawn, or give away the goods which belonged to her husband. Nor was he obliged to support her—a woman could not "bind her husband in Strictness for Necessaries." If a man died before his wife, and if no will had been made (such a will was binding even if it left a woman destitute), she did not automatically inherit all of his belongings. She legally had the rights to one-third of his land for the duration of her lifetime (she could not legally entail it to her offspring at her death unless her husband had so specified) and one-half of the rest of his estate. If there were children, her terms were reduced to one-third of her husband's estate. The rest of the property was left to male relatives—particularly to a first-born son.[8]

There are other features of the law in the early eighteenth century which emphasize the dependence and child-like status of women, and the increasingly patriarchal nature of the family. Because a married woman did not count as a responsible adult, if she lost her husband's money gambling (card playing being one of the fashionable diversions at that time) he could legally demand its return, for her wagers did not count. A woman could not be imprisoned for debt, and although a husband was responsible for her debts while she was alive, he was not legally liable upon her death.[9] Furthermore, she did not even have rights over the lives of her children. Her husband had the legal right to dispose of their children as he saw fit—where they lived, their education, their marriages, their inheritance—regardless of his wife's wishes.[10] According to a nineteenth-century legal brief prepared to defend women's right to suffrage, "until the time of Queen Elizabeth there was no sex distinction recognizable by English law." Equal political rights had been granted to all those with property qualifications, and voting had been a right "to which women equally with men were entitled and freely exercised from very ancient times. . . ."[11]

These changes in women's legal status which relegated them to the category of "children, idiots, lunatics (irresponsibles)"[12] were part of the enormous effects of the growth of capitalism on English society. They probably can be traced to the diminished economic roles played by women in the newly capitalizing economy. The expansion of cities which gathered in the displaced people of the society as a source of cheap labor, the division and professionalization of skills in the community, the separation of the place of work from the home, and above all, the evolution of a middle class in which men worked and women did not—these were the developments which phased many women out of all their former functions save the bearing of children and the management of individual households. The inability of women, particularly genteel women, to earn their own livelihood made them dependent and helpless, both in and out of fiction. They were seen as being charitably kept by their husbands and fathers, which accounts for the confusion of love and money in the novels of the period. Moll Flanders is a good example of a heroine who confuses the two: she is sure, as is Defoe, that a suitor is really in love with her only if he gives her something valuable with no strings attached.

In earlier times rural life had been cooperative. Both men and women of all classes had real economic indispensability in the households and on the land, for the economic units were self-sustaining. Common fields were shared and several households combined to work them.[13] When the enclosure acts of the seventeenth and eighteenth centuries broke down these cooperative units into smaller parcels of land, individual families were then impoverished by this separation of their economic interests. Because small farmers often could not afford the fencing costs for the enclosing of common fields, the benefits of these lands—gathering of free fuel, animal bedding, and gleaning after harvests—were no longer available.[14] These enclosure acts and the taxation of important staples made it difficult for extended families to live at the subsistence level of consuming roughly what they produced. Defoe writes of the cottage industries in rural England at the end of the seventeenth century, of the streams colored with dye from the clothmaking which individual households did for a while as a stopgap measure to supplement their meager incomes.

The poor laws further harassed and threatened the dispossessed and increased the risks entailed in eking a living from the land. J. H. Plumb writes: "Rural poverty and the fear of workhouses does much to explain the lure of the disease-ridden and dangerous life of the towns."[15] As the economy increasingly came to be based on the exchange of services and products for cash, it was no longer feasible to live in the large, loose, agricultural units where everyone shared the labor of the house and the fields. People began splitting up extended households into smaller conjugal units and moving to the cities to become shopkeepers, tradesmen, or servants. Thus were the class lines in England being restructured.

City life further destroyed the communal ties of that earlier rural life and separated people into economically independent nuclear families. One sign of this reorganization of society into isolated families is to be seen in the architectural innovations in houses during the late seventeenth century designed for individual conjugal units. There was a further specialization of space in the uses of particular rooms within these houses, guaranteeing people a hitherto unknown privacy—a condition that has its own place in the origins of fiction.[16]

As other kinds of social ties (feudal, guild, etc.) atrophied, it became more and more important to be a member of a nuclear family. Samuel Pepys referred to those under his roof as his *family* and felt responsible for all of them. Part of his ritual at the end of each year was taking stock of his family. On December 31, 1664, he writes: "My family is my wife, in good health and happy with her; her woman Mercer, a pretty, modest, quiet maid; her chambermaid Bess, her cook-maid Jane, the little girl Susan, and my boy . . . and a pretty and loving quiet family I have as any man in England." By the year of the Restoration, this was the unit of social organization in London, and when the Lord Mayor wanted to make sure there was order in the streets, he contacted through his deputies, all the male heads of families, directing them to control their house-holds.[17]

The notion of family as a small-scale model of city or even national government had wide currency, as well. "I look upon my Family as a patriarchal Sovereignty," reads one letter to *The Spectator*, "in which I am myself both King and Priest. All Great Governments are Nothing else but Clusters of these little private Royalties, and therefore I consider the Masters of Families as small Deputy-Governors presiding over the several little Parcels and Divisions of their Fellow-Subjects."[18] Although the statement is too smug and clever to ring true, as a cliché of the era it shows how the family operated as an organizing principle within the increasingly complex society. A compilation of social statistics from 1688 shows that the social milieu of the cities was one of married couples; "in London and the towns there were more married couples, more servants, more widows, and fewer children than in the country."[19] By 1696 the population estimate was based on the household rather than on the individual person.[20]

There are many signs in the culture at this time of the pressure for marrying. Men were urged to marry because it settled them into the system, making them good solid neighbors and citizens. One of the qualifications guilds looked for in a master was that he be a family man, for he was supposed to replace the apprentice's father, and be responsible for his physical and moral development. In 1724, Thomas Salmon wrote "Let the Villagers determine this Point, and tell us, if they had not rather see one Gentleman, or Clergyman, settle amongst them with a Family, than five without."[21] In 1695 a new tax levied to raise revenue for William III for the war against France taxed the heads of families for every birth, death, and marriage within their families, while bachelors and widow-ers paid an annual rate because it was assumed they could give more to the government.[22]

A pamphlet called *Marriage Promoted*, printed in 1690, listed all the reasons for marriage, both historical and current. It argued, for instance, that marriage was good for the commonwealth because it increased the population, and proposed a law obliging all men of twenty-one to marry or to pay to the government one-eighth of their yearly income each year until they did. The author cited similar laws in ancient cultures: unmarried Romans were coerced into marrying war widows; unmarried and childless Spartans were debarred from sports and forced to go naked in the marketplace. He quoted Solon against dowries, portions, jointures, "which he looked upon as *buying* of *Husbands*, and so making *Merchandize* of *Marriage*, as of other *Trades*, contrary to the Law of Nature, and first design of the Institution, which was for the *increase of Children*; hence was he wont to say, *That Men and Women should marry for Issue, Pleasure, and Love, but in no case for Money.*"[23]

The social pressure for marriage was all the more powerful on women because they were being displaced from the economic base of society. As people clustered in cities and capitalized industry grew, women became less and less central to this transformation. In 1685 one-fifth of the population of England lived in towns, and by the end of the century one-third of the population did. This urban expansion produced an increased specialization of skills; many of the traditional women's tasks were usurped by the new professional classes: doctors were replacing housewives' lore and midwifery, sewing thread was being manufactured.[24] City dwellers no longer produced what they needed for themselves, but relied more and more heavily on the production and distribution of goods by the larger community. When Defoe wrote *Robinson Crusoe* in 1719, a hero who could do everything for himself and supply his own wants without the technology of a city became a very appealing figure merely by virtue of what, a generation earlier, every family could do.

Furthermore, those industries which had been traditionally dominated by women, the food and textile industries (brewing, baking, spinning, and weaving) were increasingly taken over by men. Historically, women had done this work part-time, along with agricultural work and tending their own families. But they never formally organized into women's guilds (as the spinners did in France) or took hold of these professions legally. Since their earnings supplemented the income of their families rather than entirely supported them, they accepted small margins of profits for their labors. These unorganized, ill-paid, part-time conditions of women's work had been encouraged legally since 1363, when a statute was passed which distinguished between working men and working women. It ordered male craftsmen to choose a trade, confine themselves to it, join the appropriate guild, and work full time. "But the intent of the King and his Council is that Women, that is to say Brewers, Bakers, Carders, Spinners, and Workers as well of Wool as of Linen Cloth and of Silk, Brawdesters and Breakers of Wool and all others that do use and work all handy works may freely use and work as they have done before this time without any impeachment or being restrained by this Ordinance."[25] In other words, women were encouraged precisely *not* to organize their work professionally.

Eventually, women found themselves excluded from skilled trades because their willingness to work for lower wages on a part-time basis threatened full-time stable employment and the customary wage rates. What made final this exclusion of women from the skilled trades during the seventeenth century, was the separation of work places from living quarters. The capitalizing of hand industries—that is, the arranging of industry by middlemen who hired the labor and sold the product—demanded an expanded scale of production. They built workshops to house larger worker staffs, and divided the stages of production among them. Women, who had traditionally raised their children and tended gardens with one hand while brewing or spinning with the other, were no longer able to work professionally at trades which required their full-time presence.

A close look at the silk industry documents such an analysis. Women called "throwsters" once ran this industry, trained apprentices, and employed servants who were often male. In the course of the seventeenth century, when this work was moved from individual homes to workshops, their profits were redirected into the pockets of the managers of these workshops and the silk merchants.[26] J. H. Plumb reports this process of capitalizing occurring across the board: "it was the middlemen, the clothiers in the cloth trade, the hostmen in coal, the men who controlled the buying and selling, who had become the dominating figures in English industry in the early part of the [eighteenth] century."[27] Women were the especial casualties of this new arrangement.

Phasing women out of the new economic structures made them more and more dependent upon marrying for a living. By the late seventeenth century women's economic function had gradually shrunk to that of a *housewife*, although there had been more variety in the original occupational use of that word *wife*: fishwife, alewife, applewife, oysterwife, and so on. By the end of the eighteenth century this financial dependence seems to have been accepted as a natural state. "We as naturally look up to them [women] as the source of our pleasure," wrote a contemporary expert on women, "as they do to us as the source of their sustenance and their fortunes."[28]

The history of the word *spinster* reveals the chronology of these changes. Originally it was a term for professional women spinners, with no derogatory connotations. By 1656 it no longer had this occupational meaning, but was a legal designation: the "only addition for all unmarried women from the Viscount's Daughter Downward."[29] Women's class status was becoming less important than her marital status, and by the eighteenth century the word *spinster* had come to mean one who had no real place in the society. Not only did women take no part in the production or distribution of goods in the urban society in which they lived, but they often had very little to do with the internal economics of a household or its supervision. In other words, women had become economically superfluous both inside and outside their homes. For the first time in history, there was a class in which the men worked and the women were idle. Until then men and women of the leisured classes had entertained themselves in prescribed ways, while people of the laboring classes had worked hard, regardless of sex.[30] Within the growing urban bourgeoisie, however, men and women specialized their functions: men worked and women were supported. Tickner describes this change and dates it from about 1660:

> Unfortunately, what with the increase of wealth and the great change that came over English society with the return of Charles II . . . the outlook of the housewife changed. In many cases instead of sharing in the cares and responsibilities of the household, and in the affairs of business, the women of the upper classes began now to lead a life of leisure, which was often a very aimless one. For many women marriage became the sole preoccupation, and the preparation was rather in the direction of accomplishments which would please a man than those which were really helpful to the life of both. The education which girls received suffered in consequence. Deportment—the proper carriage of the body, aided by use of backboard and other instruments of torture—dancing and music became all-important . . . housework in too many cases became something beneath them; while, as vigorous sports were something in which no lady shared, their health deteriorated and fainting fits became somewhat common.[31]

Foreign visitors were impressed with the leisure of English women. They neither spun thread nor wove cloth nor brewed spirits nor made candles. They did not usually cook, either, for servants cooked or else food could be provided by taverns, alehouses, cookshops, piemen, food-stalls. A clerk from Strasbourg, visiting London in 1700, commented on their idleness:

Their husbands love them to such a point that they do not give them the least domestic work to do. They do not even permit them to suckle their own children. . . . Their dress is more luxurious and one sees the wives of tailors and shoemakers wearing clothes embroidered in gold or silver and adorned with gold watches. Hence the old proverb, if there was a bridge over the channel, most of the women of Europe would hasten to England.[32]

In 1748, Pehr Kalm, a Swedish naturalist visiting England wrote with astonishment about the way English women, even those living in the country, did nothing:

They never take the trouble to bake because there is a baker in every parish or village . . . the same can be said about brewing. Weaving and spinning is also in most houses a more than rare thing because their manufacturers save them from the necessity of such. . . . I confess that I at first rubbed my eyes several times to make them clear, because I could not believe I saw aright, when I first came here, out in the country, and saw the farmers' houses full of young women, while the men, on the contrary, went out both morning and evening to where the cattle were, milk-pail in hand, sat down to milk, and afterwards carried the milk pail home. . . . They are lucky in having turned the greater part of the burden of responsible management on the men, so that it is very true what both Englishmen and others write, that England is a paradise for ladies and women. It is true that the common servant girls have somewhat more work in them but still this also is moderate, and seldom goes beyond what has been reckoned up above, (cooking, washing floors, plates and dishes, darning a stocking or sewing a chemise, washing and starching linen clothes). But the mistresses and their daughters are in particular those who enjoy perfect freedom from work.[33]

Kalm goes on to describe how differently Swedish women lived their lives: how busy they were, how many responsibilities they had. In his look at England he could distinguish between servants and their mistresses because unbroken leisure for a woman was becoming a significant symbol of the status of her family; "it is become a Qualification now, to be good for no one thing in the World, but to Dance, Dress, play upon the Guitar, to prate in a Visiting-Room, or to play amongst Sharpers at Cards and Dice."[34]

It can not have been easy to exist so meaninglessly. Our best evidence of the strain exists in the records of vapours and spleen which afflicted the female population. In 1781 Dr. William Black, after reporting that in six years 29,511 women applied to Aldersgate Hospital with "Hypochondriacal disease," added

> "...it is reasonable to infer, that relaxation predominates as a female complaint *in London*. Amongst the higher, indolent, ranks, and particularly in cities, all these diseases are more frequent. The hysterical disease rarely, if ever, manifests itself before puberty and the period of menstruation, which with us is commonly about fourteen, fifteen, or sixteen: from that period to the decline of life, we may find many women single and married, subject to this infirmity. The true Hypochondriacal disease of males, and nearly analogous to the hysteria of women, is by no means so general and frequent."[35]

Even among the working classes, when women worked, it was at street-selling or washing clothes—labors which paid very much less than those of their husbands. It was very difficult for a woman to support herself, as can be seen by the extreme distress of those forced to fend for themselves. Country girls coming to the city to seek employment often found only prostitution open to them. M. Dorothy George, in her social history of London, notes the examples of women who starved to death in deserted houses and remarks: "It is significant that all the victims should have been women; there can be little doubt that the hardships of the age bore with special weight upon them."[36] There was no place in this urban society for a woman outside her father's home or her husband's home. To understand this fact makes the plight of Clarissa Harlowe more poignant.

The difficulty of being a single woman in a culture where women were assigned to their various protective males, was articulated by Mary Astell, the first English feminist. "Only let me beg to be inform'd," she asks acidly, "to whom we poor Fatherless Maids, and Widows who have lost their Masters, owe subjection. It can't be to all Men in general, unless all Men were agreed to give the same Commands; Do we then fall as Strays, to the first who finds us? By the Maxims of some Men, and the Conduct of some Women one would think so."[37] Indeed, there were so few single, self-sufficient women, that when John Evelyn ran across such a person he was so struck by her oddity that he wrote an unusually long description of her in his diary. This woman evidently lived on the four pence a day which she got from spinning and had "for many years continued a Virgin (though sought by severall to marriage) & refusing to receive any assistance of the Parish (besides the little hermitage my Lady gives her rent-free) . . . living in strange humility and contentednesse without any apparent affectation or singularity; she is continually working, or praying, or reading. . . ."[38]

Because of the exclusive dependence of a woman on her wage-earning husband in this newly urban society, his death could be a serious problem for the suddenly impoverished widow. "Experience informs us every Day," begins a pamphlet published in 1696 by The Friendly Society for Widows, "of the misery and Calamity of Women after the Death of their Husbands, which chiefly falls on such women who Marry Clergymen, Shop-Keepers, and Artificers, who tho' they may bring considerable Fortunes to their Husbands, are oftentimes left in a very Mean Condition."[39] The pamphlet goes on to propose a sort of life insurance system: each member of the Friendly Society would put a certain amount into the kitty while their husbands were alive (assuming their husbands allowed them these sums), so that a newly widowed woman might receive £500 when she needed it.

By the late seventeenth century, alternatives to marriage had been ruled out for women. Even the peaceful life of the convent was no longer possible, for when Henry VIII dissolved the religious houses, one of women's important options in the world was also dissolved. The nunneries had been equivalent institutions to monasteries. They had their own administration and sources of funds. Women in them could work their way up to positions of power and wealth; the "religious profession" was a very respectable one for a woman. When Chaucer wrote the *Canterbury Tales*, two women represented their sex: the Wife of Bath and the Prioress. They represented the two classes of women who had the funds and the independence to travel on a pilgrimage. After the English Reformation women could no longer choose to enter the scholastic and intellectual life of the convents as an alternative to marriage.

In time, nuns even came to symbolize a loss of life rather than independence or even increased spirituality. Life in the convents of the continent came to be generally pitied rather than admired. In 1716 Lady Mary Wortley Montagu wrote to a friend about an admirable woman she found in a convent in Vienna:

> I was surpriz'd to find here the only beautiful young Woman I have seen at Vienna, and not only beautifull but Genteel, witty, agreable, of a Great Family, and who had been the admiration of the Town. . . . I have been several times to see her, but it gives me too much melancholy to see so agreable a young Creature bury'd alive, and I am not surpriz'd that Nuns have often inspir'd violent passions, the pity one naturally feels for them when they seem worthy of another Destiny makeing an easy way for yet more tender sentiments. . . .[40]

Only in a society which believed that woman *ought* to be married, could Lady Mary feel this kind of pity. Certainly Chaucer's Prioress was not presented as pitiful. Interestingly, nuns came to be standard figures in many of the novels of the day—highly sexual figures, because they symbolized the longings of women locked up and waiting to be rescued from their barren futures, inspiring the "violent passions" (in their readers as well as their suitors) to which Lady Mary refers.

The convents had not only been a safe retreat, a place women could go when they left their parental homes, but they had also been the centers of learning for women, the equivalent of boarding schools. When they disbanded, women no longer had a way of acquiring an education. A pamplet written by George Wheler shows that the lack of such a place in the society was still being felt in 1698. He proposes temporary educational retreats like the old nunneries to get women off their parents' hands and to give them something of their own to do. He asks "how many families are there so burdened with Daughters their Parents cannot either for want of beauty or money, dispose of in marriage, or in any other decent manner provide for, yet are they obliged to maintain them according to their Quality till usually at their Decease they leave them without habitation and many times scarce a quarter enough to keep them decently."[41]

If women could be educated decently, they would themselves be valuable, no longer needing dowries in order to marry. "Men strive to get portion as recompense," he continued, "for taking them off their wearied Parents' hands, who after an extraordinary charge in breeding and keeping them, till, many times their age which is their ornament becomes their reproach, are forced to marry them below themselves without prospect either of credit or advantages by them."[42] He makes it clear that for economic reasons alone, parents felt compelled to marry their daughters off when they passed a certain age.

Although the economics of the marriage market were more complicated than Wheler knew, there was no doubt about the need for better educational facilities for women. In 1698 the Society for the Promotion of Christian Knowledge began to set up charity schools in England in order to extend literacy to the working class and to women. These first public schools, which came in on a wave with the English Poor Laws, part of the Protestant interest in reclaiming the poor, immoral, and lazy, were supposed to teach all children how to read and write in preparation for any future career. But the different expectations for men's and women's lives affected their education in the charity schools as well as in the best private schools. Even the daughters of wealthy parents only learned to dance and sing, play various musical instruments, make wax work, japan (i.e. lacquer), make sweetmeats and sauces, and work all kinds of needlecraft.[43] This was the best education available to rich young women, and even such limited schooling was soon ended when it was time for young ladies to shelve these unimportant amusements to enter the serious business of their lives: balls, visiting, masquerades, husband-hunting. There was good reason why Mary Astell "heard it generally complained of by very good Protestants that Monasteries were Abolished instead of being Reformed," inasmuch as they were needed to provide "a reasonable provision of education of one half of Mankind, and for a safe retreat so long and no longer than our [i.e. women's] Circumstances made it requisite."[44]

This inattention to women's education is attested to by the shocking illiteracy among even the upper class women who could afford to buy books. We know that Elizabeth Pepys could barely write. On January 31, 1663, Samuel Pepys wrote in his diary that he examined his "wife's letter intended to my Lady, and another to Mademoiselle; they were so falsely spelt that I was ashamed of them."[45] One does not know if Swift was exaggerating for the purposes of his exhortation, but in his *Letter to a Young Lady on Her Marriage* (1723) he wrote:

> It is a little hard, that not one Gentleman's Daughter in a Thousand, should be brought to read, or understand her Own Natural Tongue, or be Judge of the easiest Books that are written in it; as one may find, who can have the Patience to hear them, when they are disposed to mangle a Play or a Novel, where the least Word out of the Common Road, is sure to discontent them; and it is no wonder, when they are not so much as taught to spell in their Childhood, nor can ever attain to it in their whole lives.

Learning was so unusual in a women as to be thought of as

out of place. The culture even dictated that women be proud of their ignorance; it was part of the image of femininity. In a novel by Jane Barker a character named Galesia reflects

> how useless, or rather pernicious, Books and Learning are to our Sex. They are like Oatmeal or Charcoal to the deprav'd Appetites of Girls; for by their Means we relish not the Diversions or Imbellishments of our Sex and Station; which render us agreeable to the World, and the World to us; but live in a stoical Dulness or humersome stupidity.[46]

Swift, although he decried women's illiteracy, exhibited the ambivalence of his age in also advising his protegée that "those who are commonly called learned Women have lost all Manner of Credit by their impertinent Talkativeness and conceit of themselves."[47] Indeed, when it came down to it, he indiscriminately and satirically lumped together the published women of his own time although they did very different kinds of work.[48]

To be fair, however, there were social critics at the time who objected to this deficiency in women's education. Defoe, in his *Essay on Projects* (1697) wrote "We reproach the sex every day with folly and impertinence; while I am confident had they the advantages of education equal to us, they would be guilty of less than ourselves."[49] Mary Astell complained bitterly that women were kept from an education that would make them useful, capable of maintaining themselves economically, and give them other interests in life as their youth and looks gave way to age. She appealed to Queen Anne to provide women with an institution of monastic retirement which would employ women to teach if they did not marry, provide a refuge for "hunted heiresses," and educate those who did intend to marry so that they could educate their children and fill the gaps in their otherwise empty lives.[50]

Lady Mary Wortley Montagu, who traveled a good deal, felt that the prejudice against intellectual women in her native England was stronger than elsewhere. "To say the truth, there is no part of the world where our sex is treated with so much contempt as in England," she wrote to a friend. Lady Mary was particularly struck by the contrast of Viennese society to English society in this respect. There she found no coquettes, no prudes, no hypocrisy about sexuality. She reported that women in that society were prized, as were men, for their minds rather than for their physical attributes, whereas English society put a premium on a woman's youth and beauty, and ignored her in her riper years. "A woman till 5 and 30 is only look'd upon as a raw Girl," she writes from Vienna, "and can possibly make no noise in the world until about forty. I don't know what your Ladyship may think of this matter, but 'tis a considerable comfort to me to know there is upon earth such a paradise for old women. . . ."[51]

The religious changes in England had more to do with the changed status of women, however, than the simple fact that the Anglican churches no longer provided opportunities to them for a profession or an education. From the time that Henry VIII divorced Catherine of Aragon, the church slowly withdrew its protection of women's rights in marriage. Protestants also adopted the Old Testament feeling against women because they believed in reading the very letter of the Bible and the Bible is very explicit on the subordination of women. Not only did the patriarchal theology of Protestantism blame Eve for the primal transgression and Adam for not governing her, but it did not make much of the Virgin nor of the saints, many of whom are women. George Fox, a Quaker minister evidently rare in his belief that women were the spiritual equals of men, was aware that there were those among his followers "who do not think a woman has any more soul than a goose."[52] After he died in 1690, the character of the meetings of his congregation gradually changed. In 1701 the members began cracking down on women speaking "over much."[53] Although the Protestant belief in an individual's direct relation to God implied that women equally shared in this connection, by the end of the seventeenth century women no longer preached as they had earlier. When Susannah Wesley found herself lecturing to the crowds of people who came to hear her speak to her family during the winter of 1711 when her preacher husband was away, she was uneasy about her prerogatives. "Because of my sex, I doubt whether it be proper for me to present the prayers of the people to God," she wrote.[54]

These patriarchal attitudes naturally found their way into domestic life as well. For example, Samuel Pepys took charge of his wife's life very strictly, and was always trying to improve her. She took music lessons to please him. She had to get his permission to wear black patches when they became the fashion. He was constantly lecturing her and instilling obedience in her. On one occasion he exacted her agreement to return some pendant earrings to the shop where she had bought them, only to allow her to keep them once she had given in to him: it was the lesson rather than the money, which concerned him. Mary Astell, made particularly aware of the unequal power balance in marriage because of the notoriety of her Chelsea neighbor, the Duchess of Mazarine, who was a runaway from an unhappy marriage, observed bitterly that "however much soever Arbitrary Power may be dislik'd on a Throne, not Milton himself wou'd cry up Liberty to poor Female Slaves or plead for the Lawfulness of Resisting a Private Tyranny."[55]

Early fiction tended to reinforce these patriarchal arrangements, celebrating, as it did, the sort of romantic love which swept away all vestiges of selfhood, ideally ending in marriages which institutionalized such feeling. "I shou'd despise a Husband as much as a King who wou'd give up his own Prerogative, or unman himself to make his Wife the Head" wrote the heroine of an epistolary novel, resisting the chivalrous obeisance of a would-be lover. "We women are too weak to be trusted with Power.... Happiness in Marriage, is, where Love causes Obedience

on one side, and Compliance on the other. . . ."[56] No longer
was it a man's place selflessly to serve his lady love. That
Moll Flanders and Pamela, heroines of their respective
novels, were servants themselves reveals the new balance
between men and women in this historical period.
In a pamphlet on the causes of unhappy marriages
printed in 1739, it is suggested that this authoritarian
family organization might come as a shock to young girls
brought up on romantic notions of love, when they en-
countered the reality:

> All Women, before they are married, are accustomed to be flat-
> tered from their Infancy; are courted, attended, treated, caressed,
> and almost adored, by their Lovers, especially here in *England*;
> where we pay the greatest Deference to the Ladies of any Place in
> the World before Marriage, and the least after, of any People, who
> allow Women to be born free, as well as Men. Yesterday she was
> assured by her Lover, that his Life depended on her's. . . . But as
> soon as the Parson has pronounced the fatal Words, he puts on the
> Lord and Master. . . . This must be extremely shocking, if we allow
> Women capable of any Reflexion. . . .[57]

This state of affairs was intensified in the case of wives
who were still really children. Pamela, it will be remembered, was fifteen years old. A tale in *The Spectator* tells of
a widow who was first married off at fourteen years of age.
Her husband, she said, "looked upon me as a meer Child,
he might breed up after his own Fancy."[58] Samuel Pepys
was twenty-three and his wife fifteen when they married;
John Evelyn was twenty-seven and his wife twelve. A few
months after the wedding, with no intervening word about
his new bride, Evelyn notes in his diary that he is returning
to England to settle some affairs, his "Wife being yet very
Young . . . .left under the care of an excellent Lady and
Prudent Mother."[59] This age disparity inevitably rein-
forced the masculine absolutism of the household.[60]
One of the more significant expressions of men's dominion was their control of women's sexuality. According to
Ian Watt, "In the history of mankind strictness in sexual

relations tends to coincide with the increasing importance
of private property. . . ."61 This connection is taken for
granted by a historian of the period, with an unquestioning
eighteenth-century attitude towards ownership and property. "Is it Liberty to have all the Women of the World in
common?" he asks. "A Liberty to invade every Man's
Property, as Occasion Offers? Or would they have no such
thing as Property in this Case? Can they suppose that the
most desireable Creatures in Nature would occasion no
Contention, when every other Trifle does, where Property
is not settled?"62 An extreme example of this attitude
appears in a story told around London:

> A certain Woman finding her End draw near, bethought herself of
> asking her Husband's Pardon for a great Injury she had done him,
> and with which she would acquaint him, in case he promis'd to
> forgive her. He readily comply'd, and then she own'd an Affair of
> Gallantry; the Husband assur'd her that he would not resent it,
> adding withal, that he had done her some Wrong, for which he
> ask'd Pardon, this she did willingly, being no less surprized, than
> transported with her Husband's extraordinary Goodness. Upon
> this he own'd to her that he was well appriz'd of her Conduct,
> which had made him poison her.63

The stress on this woman's chastity is presented here as a
straightforward matter of property relations, rather than
jealous love or protectiveness or any other human relation
of the man to his wife. He kills her as one might shoot a
lame animal, when it can no longer function as it is meant
to in the world.

That sexual activity was a question of property rights
rather than of mutual fidelity is also clear in Lord Halifax's
famous letter to his daughter (1678) in which he sets down
the double standard as clearly as it has ever been stated:
"Frailties . . . [are] in the utmost degree *Criminal* in the
Woman, which in a *Man* passeth under a much *gentler
Censure*." He adds that "next to the danger of *committing*
the Fault to your self, the greatest is that of *seeing* it in your
Husband. . . . Besides, it is so coarse a Reason which will

be assign'd for a Lady's too great Warmth upon such an occasion, that Modesty no less than Prudence ought to restrain her; since such an indecent Complaint makes a Wife much more ridiculous, than the Injury that provoketh her to it." He explains that "The Root and the Excuse of this Injustice is the Preservation of Families from any Mixture which may bring a Blemish to them: And whilst the *Point of Honor* continues to be so plac'd, it seems unavoidable to give your *Sex*, the greater share of the Penalty."[64]

What he means, of course, is that women's sexuality must be exercised in the services of family property rights. As a mother explains to her daughter in a model letter in Richardson's *Letters . . . on Important Occasions*, a man's illegal offspring cannot inherit whereas a woman's illegal offspring can.[65] Therefore the possible injury a wife can do her husband is much greater than the injury he can do her, if one values property and the lines of its transfer.

As women's function in society diminished to the obvious reproductive one, they were increasingly thought of in exclusively sexual terms. No longer did their labors earn them a place in the larger community; only their sex did. And although caught between the necessity of marrying for a livelihood and the expectations of decorous modesty, they began to make better use of their "charms" as bait to catch husbands. John Evelyn noted in his diary the first time that London women "began to paint themselves, formerly a most ignominious thing, and used only by prostitutes."[66] By the end of the seventeenth century the amount of oils, rouges, perfumes, and cosmetics being sold was dizzying.[67] Mary Astell articulated the difference between "the making their Fortune, as Men call it; or with us Women the setting ours to sale, and the dressing forth our selves to purchase a Master; and when we have got one, that which we very improperly term our business, the Oeconomy of his and our own Vanity and Luxury, or Covetousness, as the humor happens, has all the application of our Minds. . . ."[68] To be sure, this is an expression of her piety as much as her feminism, for she felt that they entailed each other. She was always exhorting her audience to turn away from worldly vanity for she felt that it particularly (and perniciously) dominated women's lives. The degree to which women primped and dressed and ornamented themselves, a practice which had only begun in earnest during the Restoration, is indicated by the amount of space devoted to fashion in papers like the *Spectator, Tatler,* and *Guardian.* It was standard practice, for instance, to poke good-natured fun at attempts at fashion in provincial towns outside of London. Inasmuch as this preoccupation also reflected class, it was shared by men as well. Pepys devotes many pages of his diary to his own fashionable accoutrements. But the importance of attracting a husband made dress a prime concern in a woman, and no small part of her accomplishments. *The Spectator* admires the wit of a man who speaks of dressing as an expressive art for a woman. He notices an elegant young lady at the theater and remarks to his companion that "her Dress is very becoming, but the Merit of that Choice is owing to her Mother; for though. . .I allow a Beauty to be as much commended for the Elegance of her Dress, as a Wit for that of his Language; yet if she has stolen the colour of her Ribbands from another, or had Advice about her Trimmings, I shall not allow her the Praise of Dress any more than I would call a Plagiary an Author."[69] Such connoisseurship could only evolve in a civilization in which women were brought up for display.

A work reporting on the *Present State of Matrimony* claimed that the young women of the early eighteenth century were "wiser, and more knowing in the Arts of Coquetry, Galantry, and other Matters relating to the Difference of Sexes etc. before they come to be Twenty, than our Great-Grandmothers were in all their Lives."[70] Perhaps some of these strategies for sexual self-dramatization were learned from descriptions of the tactics of heroines in novels, where many women make good use of their seductiveness, like this one invented by Eliza Haywood, who, like a soldier inspecting her weapons, "consulted her Glass after what Manner she should Dress, her Eyes, the gay, languishing, the sedate, the commanding, the beseeching Air were put on, a thousand times and as often rejected; and she had scarce determined which to make use of. . . ."[71]

It is undeniably true that whenever the novels of the period are about women, they are about the politics of their sexuality: avoiding premarital sexual traps, fencing with suitors, catching husbands, leaving the father's home for a husband's home or, as some of the plots suggest, turning the father's home into a husband's home. Indeed, there are really an unexpected number of incest tales which turn up in these early novels, perhaps a sign of the difficulty of unproblematic access between the sexes. Some of these are tales of brother-sister incest, but the relationship is more often between a young woman and an older man, often married, who acts as a father in relation to the heroine. These seductive relationships to authority figures, either fathers or guardians, were appropriate fantasies for women with so little power over their own lives and so little experience with any but the all-powerful males of their own families.

So many novels tell this same story (was not Mr. B. the authority in Pamela's life?) that the point is worth stressing by examining several more closely. In *Love in Excess* the young and virginal heroine Melliora is in love with her guardian Count d'Elmont and he secretly loves her in return. After some complicated machinations set up by d'Elmont's jealous wife, he ends up killing his wife (accidently of course), freeing himself to marry Melliora at the end.[72] In *Secret Memoirs . . . from New Atalantis*, another lascivious guardian falls in love with his ward, who is the daughter of a friend. She hugs and kisses him (while calling him "papa") until his passion overcomes his scruples. He decides to use books to deprave her mind and weaken her sense of honor. Leading her to the library, "he took down an Ovid, and opening it just at the love of Myra for her Father, conscious red overspread his Face; he gave it to her to read. . . ."[73] Sometimes the outlines are more subterranean, as in *The Fatal Secret* where a man driven by lust drugs and rapes a woman who is, unknown to him, his own daughter-in-law.[74] In Marivaux' *The Life of Marianne* the young girl's first protector Mr. Climal, from whom she expects the kindness of a father, shocks her by trying to seduce her. She manages to get out of his clutches after much difficulty and runs away to a nunnery. This book, in fact, is structured very much like Richardson's *Pamela*, for the young innocent has no protection against the designing world but the strength of her virtue.[75]

The Unnatural Mother and Ungrateful Wife has an extreme version of this plot.[76] A young orphan girl, taken into the home of a happy couple, comes between the kindly maternal woman and her husband. Slowly she takes over the prerogatives of the household, bullying the first wife into sickness and then death. She marries the man, but before long a young and handsome doctor catches her eye. Next she manages to have her first husband committed; however, she is finally thwarted when her own daughter steals away the handsome young doctor and leaves the unnatural mother and ungrateful wife to die raving mad, a fitting ending for a woman who showed so much sexual appetite, and so much will.

Nor was this so unusual a configuration: many of these fictions are propelled by tensions implicit in the mother-father-daughter triangle. Often, too, the daughter wins the competition, in much the same way that young men in male oedipal stories defeat aging champions or outwit older rivals, pitting their young energy and desire against the experience of an older generation. In these epistolary tales, heroines prove their prowess by managing to attract wealthy and powerful lovers from their rivals. (The charming exception to this paradigm is *The British Recluse* (1722), in which two women decide to retire to the country and live together, after comparing notes on the grand passions of their lives only to discover that they have both loved the same man.) Probably this recurrent theme of competitive sexuality reflected the pressures of the marriage market as much as any psychosexual formula.

That women set about determinedly to marry in life as well as in fiction is visible in the economic arrangements of marriage, in the amount of money families were willing to pay in order to marry off their daughters. By the end of the seventeenth century, the price of husbands was increasing. That is, women were bringing more money into marriage as dowries, and having less settled on them as their allowance in the marriage contracts as jointure, than in earlier times. In 1650 women had roughly 100 pounds of jointure settled on them for every 600 pounds of dowry. By the end of the century the ratio had become 100 pounds of jointure to every 1000 pounds of dowry.[77] "There are some now living in these kingdoms, that remember when Money was the least part considered in *Marriage*," wrote a polemicist who objected to the way venal considerations interfered with plentiful childbearing, "when that *Summ* would have been thought a Fortune for a *Lord*, that is now despised by a *Merchant*; yet then there were few dyed without *Posterity.* . . ."[78]

It is hard to tell if the changing dowry/jointure ratio reflects a tighter marriage market, and therefore is a sign of increased demand for husbands for middle- and upper-class women, or if it is one of the causes of that tighter marriage market and therefore originates in other economic conditions of the time. One explanation is that the development of a cash economy in England was forcing the land-poor nobility to marry middle-class money. Since they were not part of the capitalist cash flow, the only way they could raise the money they needed to buy the new consumer goods or cover the cost of rising taxes was to marry money in the mercantile class. This was the state of affairs illustrated in Jane Austen's *Persuasion*, which opens with scenes of a baronet who must retrench because he no longer has the ready cash to keep himself and his establishment in style and he has no other resources. The kind of legal transfer of property, the strict settlement, which kept stable political power in a family made these landed aristocrats virtual prisoners of their property. Estates were entailed to the possible offspring at the time of marriage settlements. This meant that the owner was merely the life-tenant of the property and could not raise cash by selling or mortgaging even a small part of it. Cash had to be found in a marriage partner. Middle-class women with dowries were supposed to carry money with them, like bees carrying pollen, to enrich the upper classes.

Another reason for marrying wealth was that marriage itself was becoming a more costly undertaking. Living fashionably in London, even part of the year, was getting to be expensive in this conspicuous society. In *The Batchelor's Estimate of the Expenses of a Married Life* (1725), Edward Ward warns a friend who wants to marry a woman with a fortune of 2,000 pounds that city taxes, servants, clothes, and the expenses of having children will eat up her fortune in no time.

Although marriage in the past had always been a matter of alliances between families for their mutual advantage, this crassly acquisitive nature of marriage was new, and was without the rationale of enlarged community, political or military security, generational continuity, ritual or religious significance, or any of the other reasons which had previously distinguished the institution of marriage. Karl Marx places the new economic underpinning of marriage with its property relation and exclusive attitude in relation to other families among the changes of this period:

> In the eighteenth century the concept of the family was abolished by philosophers, because the actual family was already in the process of dissolution, at the highest pinnacles of civilization. The internal family bond was dissolved, the separate components constituting the concept of family were dissolved, for example, obedience, piety, fidelity in marriage, etc.; but the real body of the family, the property relation, the exclusive attitude in relation to

other families, forced cohabitation,—relations produced by the existence of children, the structure of modern towns, the formation of capital, etc.—all these were preserved, although with numerous violations, because the existence of the family had been made necessary by its connection with the mode of production that exists independently of the will of bourgeois society.[79]

Marx here is attempting to define two meanings of *family*: one in its commendable, spiritual sense as the extended bond of feudal times; the other as an economic unit. He points out that in the eighteenth century the first meaning of family gave way to more blatant materialistic considerations.

Thus, although the family was even more important as an economic entity than ever before, there was an ever-widening gap between the stated social and human reasons for its existence and the real material level at which it functioned. This is what makes the opening scenes in *Clarissa* so painful. Clarissa's family bands together against her in greed. They submerge their affection for her in their capitalistic desire to consolidate and enlarge their estate. Love, respect, and compassion are all subjugated to her parents' materialism. Her father uses family and marriage as a business venture. And caught in this world in which all people, even family, have their price, Clarissa still will not sell.

The economic realities of the day must have presented actual problems of this sort, for dilemmas like Clarissa Harlow's, marriage for reasons of family estate versus marriage for love, keep turning up in the fiction. Occasionally the other side of the question is also presented. In *The Polite Correspondence* there is case made for submitting oneself to family expectations, by a woman who is upset because her son wants to marry where there is no fortune. Evidently the family estate brings in very little money, not enough to support another household should the inheritor marry while the owner is still alive. This writer, whose

dowry has never been paid in full, does not want the family
fortunes to go under; and in the marriage choice of her son
she sees the difference between a run-down, debt-ridden
estate and one which is flourishing and growing:

> I am very sensible that my Father has just Reason to be extremely
> chagrin'd at this ill tim'd Match; you know well enough that his
> Estate is called six hundred Pounds a Year, but I have heard him
> say, that he thinks it a good Year when it brings him four hundred
> into his Pocket, he had no great Opportunity of laying up, and
> therefore the Marriage of his Son would not have been very
> agreeable, even if he had met with a good Match. Judge you then
> how much he must be incumber'd, now this Boy had thrown
> himself away, and he is indebted to Florimond three thousand
> Pounds for my Fortune: It is true, my Spouse will never ask for it,
> but still the Sense of the Debt will remain heavy on the good old
> Man's Mind, and the Knowledge of this makes me so heartily
> uneasy, that I almost wish myself single. It is now that I perceive
> how unjust a Thing it is for Children to marry according to their
> own Caprice, and by one indiscreet Action, baffle all the Care of a
> Parents Life. I cannot however help thinking that this Doctrine
> ought to be particularly considered by Sons who are to inherit the
> Estates, and ought therefore to support the honour of Families.[80]

It is a very talky passage and the full economic details so
obviously interest the writer (and the audience, one
assumes) that one understands how inextricably such complex financial considerations were part of family feeling on
romance and marriage. Certainly the history of marriages
arranged for practical reasons was longer than those arranged for love, which was a relatively new complication to
the whole problem. Courtly love, which became part of the
culture after the twelfth century, never ended in marriage.
Rather, it was thought of as that heightened state of feeling
which went with adulterous relationships and was not
appropriate to the serious undertaking of marriage.
Héloise, for instance, did not want to ruin her relationship
with her lover Abelard by marrying him; Abelard's sister
asked him "But can you be sure Marriage will not be the
Tomb of her Love?"[81] Nobody yet believed the mythical

ending of love stories: "they were married and lived happily ever after."

These attitudes had changed by the end of the seventeenth century; by then love had become a radical reason for marriage. Along with the necessity for women to marry came a new belief in the possibility of romantic marriage. Although the economic odds were more heavily weighted against women, now there was a trump card which could annihilate all advantages; "the Power of Love, that Leveller of Mankind; that blender of Distinction and Hearts."[82] Because love crossed class boundaries and allied families which hitherto would have had no connection with one another, love now had real economic and social consequences for the first time.

The new imperative of *love* made it possible for upwardly mobile middle-class families to marry into the closed aristocracy or for impoverished nobility to replenish their estates by matching their younger sons with the daughters of the rich bourgeoisie. This intermarrying of classes is documented by Defoe in *The Compleat English Gentleman* (1730) where he demonstrates the mixture of money and blood in the antecedents of some of the leading families of his day. These movements across class lines had not been possible earlier when money and rank were in the same hands, and matches were made, like alliances, between powers.

Because marriage was an important avenue of mobility, members of the middle class groomed their daughters for marriage to members of the elite. Noble women never married down. As Mr. B. explained to his sister Lady Danvers in *Pamela*, women could be elevated to their husband's status, although a lower-class husband could only drag his wife down. Even lower-class parents tried to expose their daughters to the manners of gentlewomen (cf. *Moll Flanders*) to increase the chances of their daughters marrying up—the ultimate accomplishment to which a woman could aspire. Thus besides promulgating the new myth of romantic love lasting a lifetime, the function of novels of this period was to demonstrate the skills necessary for ambitious young women to land husbands, and to coach them in upper-class manners, presented long scenarios of aristocratic gesture and speech. The last half of *Pamela* is not only an education for the heroine in her new status, but also for Richardson's class-conscious readership, interested in what changing one's class literally entailed.

Everybody spoke to the question of marriage for money and class versus marriage for love. It was a significant dispute of the time; novels focused on it, the popular journals were full of it. Practically every issue of *The London Magazine* had several stories concerning the effects, good and bad, of marrying where parental pressure directed rather than where desire inclined. *The Spectator* often printed pieces exploring different reasons for marrying, and generally favored love as the best motivation.[83] On the other hand, Defoe, in *Conjugal Lewdness*, advised against marrying out of one's class because class snobbery could ruin the relationship.[84] Fictions turning on the conflict between love and money often treated it as a generational confrontation: the young pressed for love while the older generation adhered to their more practical credo. But considerations of status and property were seen as corrupt motivations by the liberal sentimentalists of the day. In this newer code, the first priority lay in forming an attachment based on passionate love, scornfully setting aside any material consideration which opposed this reason for marriage.

Because of these marriages across class lines, with their attendant social and economic consequences, the marriage laws had to be made stricter. Matrimony was becoming too important to be defined as loosely as in times when this relationship did not shift rank and money around. Henry VIII's divorce of Catherine of Aragon had moved marriage from the inviolable realm of the sacred to a more flexible, contractual basis on which ecclesiastical courts could rule.

Thus it had the effect of making marriage a rather vague affair, legally speaking, until the middle of the eighteenth century when a civil marriage law was finally passed. Until then, marriage could be accomplished by a single exchange of vows—the presence of clergy was not even necessary. The basis of marriage was simply the assent of the two people involved, without any further religious consecration. In cases of contested consummated marriages, the ecclesiastical courts, which had the right to uphold or nullify them, generally blessed these pre-contracts.[85]

The inadequacy of the law and the inexactness with which marriage was legally defined explain the sequence in which Richardson's Pamela nimbly avoids being tricked into a fraudulent marriage with Mr. B. The lack of clarity in the law made possible many exploitations. There were, for instance, the notorious marriages of Fleet Street, where women were taken and married for the sake of seduction, or their fortunes, or both, and then deserted. Because a woman's property reverted automatically to her husband upon marriage, many wealthy young ladies were fair game for smooth-tongued adventurers who convinced them to elope, to marry for love, against their parents' wishes.[86] Here, too, women went to marry to evade their debts,[87] or parish overseers went to marry off pauper women in order to remove them from the public rolls and put the burden of maintenance on someone else. Here, records of marriages could be created or erased, all for a price.

Finally the government stepped in and ended these abuses. Marriage had become too important in the society not to have some kind of clearly defined legal status. In 1753 Lord Hardwicke's Marriage Act was passed. It was the government's first attempt to regulate marriage in England; until then, marriage was a religious rather than a civil concern. The new law not only required publishing banns at least two to seven days before the ceremony, but also stated that the ceremony had to take place in the local chapel of the parish where at least one of the parties had lived for four weeks. The officiating parson did not have to obtain the parents' consent; it was the parents' place to register their dissent with him if they disapproved. If the parties were under twenty-one years of age, parental dissent made the marriage void; if the parties were over twenty-one, they could petition for a legal marriage despite parental disapproval; all marriages were to be recorded on "proper books of vellum or good durable paper."[88] Thus, a complete set of records of marriage in England dates from 1753. The penalty for evading any of these strictures was death. By the middle of the eighteenth century, conjugal relations had become a matter for criminal punishment. As a property relation, marriage was governed by the same laws that governed theft.

The stated legal purpose of the Marriage Act was "for the better Preventing Clandestine Marriages" with the implication that the government was taking care, with missionary zeal, to protect the morals of the lower classes who married promiscuously. This was particularly true, evidently, of sailors whose shore leaves were often a good deal shorter than the four weeks stipulated in the Marriage Act. But a well-reasoned pamphlet of the day argues that this Act was actually designed to curb the kinds of marriages which were drastically altering the face of English society:

> It is alledged, in Support of this Bill, that it is to prevent *imprudent* Marriages; by which I suppose are *principally* meant such Matches as are made by Parties, between whom there is a great Disparity in point of Fortune, or Station in Life. But that such Marriages are *political* Evils, is far from being true, for I take it to be a good and just Maxim, founded on the Observations of many great and learned Politicans, that the Wealth of a Nation ought to be as *equally* divided among the inhabitants *as may be*. . . .
>
> The general Outcry against unequal Matches arises more from either private Interest or the Pride of Family (a Disposition in no wise worthy of publick Encouragement) than from a Regard to the Commonweal.[89]

This radical writer goes on to say that this law not only discriminates against the poor and the vagrant, but against women. For no longer would promises have the ecclesiastical sanctity of commitment once there were further legal requirements for marriage, and so "Men may promise with more Impunity, and the injured Fair is in great Danger of becoming useless to Society as to the Propagation of legitimate Issue, and he that has ruined her has an Opportunity to triumph over her Credulity. . . ."[90] Whatever revolutionary notions this writer has about the distribution of wealth, he still firmly makes the assumption of his culture that once a woman has engaged in sexual activity out of wedlock, she is ruined; this follows from his other premise, that her chief purpose in life is the production of "legitimate Issue." He further assumes that women want to marry more than men do, and that men will go to any lengths to trick a woman into bed. These were attitudes which no one disputed.

These, then, are the economic, social and even institutional changes which form the context of the developing novel. They are the forces which affected women's place in English society and which created a new kind of heroine, defined almost entirely by her relation to men, struggling for integrity and happiness in a world in which she was entirely dependent on other people. Women had become pawns in the game of economic redistribution without being recognized as full, productive members of the community which used them this way. To understand this is to understand that the sometimes silly and repetitive fiction of the period was an expression of an unhealthy state of affairs in the culture. This fiction found its ideal form in letters because of the psychological and literary implications of letters. Therefore, we will next examine the popularity of letter collections and the fictive qualities of such collections which evolved into the novels of the early eighteenth century.

3

The Social Context
of Letters

The epistolary fiction which was published and read in
England in the early eighteenth century came out of a
culture which took the letter seriously. Any theorizing
about the epistolary novel must take this fact into account:
the letter in the eighteenth century had a special place in
the intellectual and personal lives of literate people. Communication by written word was the only contact between
people living at a distance from one another and letters
were greatly prized in those times of bad roads and slow
vehicles. One historian of the letter notes that it cost as
much as six shillings to deliver a letter outside of London,
paid by the receiver. At a rate like that, the writing of a
letter had to be taken seriously. He goes on to say that even
"in a world in which other forms of news and entertainment were scanty, slow, and unreliable, it remains surprising that even poor people should have been willing—as
clearly they were—to pay so much for what, to us, seems
sometimes so little."[1]

In 1660 an act established the national Post Office.
Twenty years later the service was extended, prices came
down, and stamps were introduced. The new penny post
service set up 334 houses for receiving letters and reached

as many as 200 towns outside of London.[2] By 1725 Defoe was enthusing about the penny post service within London:

> The Penny Post, a modern Contrivance of a private Person, one Mr. William Dockraw, is now made a Branch of the general Revenue by the Post Office; and though, for a Time, it was subject to Miscarriages and Mistakes yet now it is come also into so exquisite a Management, that nothing can be more exact and 'tis with the utmost safety and Dispatch that Letters are delivered at the remotest Corners of the Town, almost as soon as They could be sent by a Messenger and that from Four, Five, Six to Eight times a Day, according as the Distance of the Place makes it practicable.[3]

The receiver paid one penny for any letter delivered within the city; if it was to go further, both receiver and sender paid a penny each. One could safely send money by post, or packages weighing as much as a pound. The penny post was admired by visitors from other countries who recognized this service as one of the significant accomplishments of the English, and a great advantage of London life.[4]

Educated people were expected to know how to write graceful letters, how to compose their thoughts on paper. Schools trained this skill—letter-writing was a standard composition assignment, and students read and copied from classical examples.[5] Londoners must have been accustomed to writing them, for *The Spectator* reports a steady stream of letters addressed to the editor: "I have Complaints from Lovers, Schemes for Projectors, Scandal from Ladies, Congratulations, Compliments, and Advice in abundance"[6] —testimony to the readiness with which readers took pen in hand to scribble off their reactions to even so impersonal a target as that popular daily.

This impulse to write autobiographically also comes out of the older Puritan tradition of noting the facts of an individual's life, gathering up the fragments of his or her character in action. Many people wrote regularly in diaries and journals on the theory that God's Divine Purpose could be discerned in the shape of a person's life, visible in the daily details of emotions and events. Diary-keeping also served as a kind of intellectual self-inspection in the Age of Reason which believed that "knowledge of its own activity, intellectual self-examination, and foresight are the proper function and essential task of thought."[7] Such are the intentions, for example, announced at the beginning of one of the many diaries which have come down to us from that time:

> I intend particularly to observe my own temper and state of mind as to my fitness and disposition for study or the easiness or satisfaction it finds within itself and the particular cause of that or of the contrary uneasiness that often disturbs my mind. . . . I shall be able then to review any parts of my life, have the pleasure of it if it be well spent, if otherwise know how to mend it. It will help me to know myself better and give a better judgement of my own ability and what I am best qualified for. I shall know what best suits my own temper, what is most likely to make me easy and contented and what the contrary.[8]

There is not a hint of doubt about the appropriateness of his plan in this sturdy beginning; self-examination seems healthy and possible rather than vain, solipsistic, illusory.

The fact is that whether or not the literate were writing about themselves in journals, diaries, memoirs, or letters, and the period is full of these forms, sufficient quantities of paper were being bought, scribbled on, and circulated for the government to tax it as a source of national revenue. The Stamp Act of 1711 imposed a tax on "stamped vellum, parchment and paper, and upon certain printed papers, pamphlets and advertisements."[9] That means that more business and personal correspondence was carried on in writing than ever before, and that people spent more time sitting alone, writing to their fellow creatures rather than carrying on their business directly, in person.

Not surprisingly then, the kind of books this literate public enjoyed were collections of letters. There were letters of travelers *en route*, letters of spying and political intrigue, love letters, letters satirizing social conditions or caricaturing types, letters telling interesting stories, letters from famous people, letters from plain anonymous people. Some made serious claims to authenticity while others did not, and they often were collected without regard to this difference. It is also difficult to make generalizations about the subject matter of these collections, for the letters are usually written on every conceivable subject and in most volumes are discontinuous, each one speaking to a different situation. The editor of *The Spectator* gives a clear sense of the indiscriminate inclusion in these volumes:

> I have often thought, that if the several Letters which are Written to me under the Character of *Spectator,* and which I have not made use of, were published in a Volume, they would not be an unentertaining Collection. The Variety of the Subjects, Stiles, Sentiments, and Informations, which are transmitted to me, would lead a very curious, or very idle Reader, insensibly along through a great many Pages. I know some Authors, who would pick up a *Secret History* out of such Materials, and make a Bookseller an Alderman by the Copy.[10]

What he describes here is really no different from the miscellanies which did find favor with "curious" and "idle" readers, collections of letters with no common theme, save their form. And although not every bookseller was assured of making his fortune on secret histories, readers loved best of all, those letters which they believed were not intended for public scrutiny.

In addition to these collections which appeared to be written for posting, there were also a number of letter-writing manuals put together to instruct the populace on the proper wording of letters for various occasions as well as the appropriate sentiments informing them. Both the entertaining and the instructive collections often included translations of letters by past masters (Voiture, Cicero, etc.) to show the heights which the art of letter writing was capable of reaching. Indeed, the demand for such style books can be seen in the way that early epistolary novels capitalized on their titles: *The Polite Correspondence* (a novel possibly by John Campbell) sounds like a collection or a manual, and *The Lover's Secretary* (the second title to *The Adventures of Lindamira*) not only sounds like one, but was the title of a miscellaneous collection of love letters which came out in 1692.

Letter collections were also piling up in booksellers' shops because the letter was a perfect form for the new breed of hack writers working long, cramped hours for miserable pay on Grub Street. For the most part, writers sold their work outright to booksellers and had to keep turning out new material in order to keep eating. Letters were short and easy to write; formulae which worked could be endlessly repeated with minor variations. Most writers tried to write more lucrative plays, worth three or four times as much as novels[11], but more often managed letter fiction in which one sees traces of drama: dramatic monologues masquerading as letters, Elizabethan comedy situations with disguised identities and forgeries,[12] and stories of cuckoldry straight from the Restoration stage. Letters could be quickly adapted to the needs of the authors and booksellers, and the public kept buying them.

The career of Thomas Brown, an educated gentleman who resorted to his pen for a livelihood at the turn of the century, illustrates the degree to which commercial writers leaned on the marketable letter. Brown did not write for the sake of Art; as a contemporary said of him: "he did not consult his own liking so much as his Booksellers, and took such as they offer'd the best Price for. . . ."[13] They must have offered good prices for letters, because Brown's *Collected Works* are filled with them. He translated the master letter-writers: Pliny, Cicero, Aristaenetus, Voiture; he edited the familiar letters of the Earl of Rochester; he composed exemplary letters for standard occasions requiring appropriate responses; he wrote facetious letters to air his satiric views on a variety of issues, using them to make elaborate jokes or tell brief stories. For example, his

Letters From the Dead to the Living are humorous comments on the contemporary scene written by well-known, recently dead characters of his day.[14] So popular that several other writers (including Defoe) tried to capitalize on the title, *Letters From the Dead to the Living* went through several editions immediately, insuring Brown's reputation with his contemporaries. Most historians of the period also attribute to him one of the earliest full-fledged epistolary novels, the delightful *Adventures of Lindamira*.[15]

Because women's writing had a special place in the development of epistolary fiction, this novel of letters from the pen of Lindamira was plausible to the reading public. Letters were the one sort of writing women were supposed to be able to do well. Literate women wrote letters even in the days when they put pen to paper for no other reason, and so the public was ready to buy volumes of letters published under a woman's name. By the early eighteenth century there were at least two collections of epistolary prose by women in wide circulation: the *CCXI Sociable Letters* by Margaret Cavendish, the eccentric Duchess of Newcastle, and various unauthorized translations from the letters of Madame de Sévigné. Virginia Woolf's essay about Dorothy Osborne's wonderful letters to William Temple notes that letter writing was the mode of expression appropriated by women writers *en route*, so to speak, to professional authorship. "Had she been born in 1827, Dorothy Osborne would have written novels;" says Woolf, "had she been born in 1527 she never would have written at all. But she was born in 1627, and at that date though writing books was 'ridiculous for a woman' [as Dorothy Osborne said of the Duchess of Newcastle when she dared to write and publish her *CCXI Sociable Letters*] there was nothing unseemly in writing a letter."[16] Furthermore, letter writing could be made to fit in with the scope and expectations of a woman's life. "It was an art that could be carried on at odd moments, by a father's sick-bed among a thousand interruptions, without exciting comments, anonymously as it were, and often with the pretense that it served some useful purpose." [17]

Letters were an important line of communication with the outside world at this time when women led rather cloistered lives. Men lived gregariously, in the company of their fellows in the coffee houses and inns of the city: "these Coffee-houses are the constant Rendezvous for Men of Business as well as the idle People, so that a Man is sooner ask'd about his Coffee-house than his Lodging."[18] Not so with women. They were excluded from those centers of social exchange because it was not considered respectable for them to appear in public places (as Lord Halifax warned his daughter) and because, as Dudley Ryder wrote, it was not in their interest to be too accessible:

> Young women should be kept at a proper distance and not allow themselves in too close and near a correspondence with our sex. Their beauty or other less qualifications grow familiar before matrimony and we grow tired and weary of them before we have gained the effect of them.[19]

So women generally stayed at home writing letters which were at once a way of being involved with the world while keeping it at a respectable arm's length. Correspondence became the medium for weaving the social fabric of family and friendships in letters of invitation, acceptance, news, condolence, and congratulations.

Letters were the perfect vehicle for women's highly developed art of pleasing, for in writing letters it is possible to tailor a self on paper to suit the expectations and desires of the audience. This is why they were used not only to transmit conventional messages, but also to maintain the proper distance in more ticklish situations. Lady Mary Wortley Montagu, for instance, wrote letters to her father while still living at home, arguing with him respectfully for a marriage of her own preference. Similarly, letters were the place to have skirmishes with lovers and suitors, for they drew the battle lines at a safe remove from the actual person of the modest woman. Through letters, a woman could hold her place in a network of almost fictitious connections and relationships which were maintained primarily on paper.

Because so many private relationships came to be conducted in letters, especially for home-bound women, these exchanges came to be understood as the repository for emotions usually enclosed by convention, the place to look for records of a person's secret doings. Booksellers often advertised the fact that a set of letters had not been intended for publication because privacy, like virginity, invites violation. They traded on the implication that letters could give a more unguarded, natural picture of a life than memoirs which were written with a public audience in mind. Thus, the title page of one of Curll's productions—a little volume called *Letters, Poems, and Tales: Amorous, Satyrical and Gallant which passed between Several Persons of Distinction* (1718)—advertises itself as the complete contents "found in the Cabinet of that celebrated Toast Mrs. Long, since her Decease." Curll must have counted on the implied exposure of a lady of fashion (whom Swift thought "the most beautiful Person of the Age she lived in, of great Honor and Virtue, Infinite Sweetness and Generosity of Temper, and the true Good Sense")[20] for there is nothing in the scattered and miscellaneous contents of the volume to recommend it. The letters of another woman, the writer Mary Delariviere Manley, although sold to a bookseller named Bragg when she needed the money,[21] are deceptively introduced by a dedicatory epistle which asks her pardon "for venturing to make anything of yours publick, without your leave." The bookseller goes on to head off her imagined objection saying that "these Letters which I expose, were not proper for the Publick; the Droppings of your Pen, fatigu'd with

Thought and Travel. . . ."[22] The language is a come-on tempting the reader to see the real Mrs. Manley up close.

Sometimes the effect of privacy was achieved by assuring the reader that the writer was a person of quality, and consequently worthy of attention, although the actual names had to be blanked out or disguised so as to protect the Persons whose letters were being distributed so indecorously. It was considered indecent to have one's letters published—so much so that Pope went to a great deal of trouble to hush up his part in the first printing of his letters. He was, in fact, the first literary figure whose private letters were published during his own lifetime and at his own instigation.[23] To protect his respectability, and because he knew how much the public valued private letters, he tried to make it appear that they had been innocently composed without the expectation of public fame, and that they had been stolen from him. This is the disingenuous statement he printed with this volume of letters:

> Many of them having been written on the most trying occurences, and all in the openness of friendship, are a proof what were his real Sentiments, as they flow'd warm from the heart, and fresh from the occasion; without the least thought that ever the world should be witness to them. Had he sat down with a design to draw his own Picture, he could not have done it so truly; for whoever sits for it (whether to himself or another) will inevitably find the features more compos'd, than his appear in these letters.[24]

The promise to reveal the true picture of the writer, too often hidden beneath the necessary social artifices, is typical of the claims of letter collections in this era. The whole point of a collection like *The Post-Boy Rob'd of His Mail*, no less than of Pope's pretended "robbed mail," was to uncover people's unadorned attitudes, as the first letter makes clear:

> Letters were the pulling off the Mask in a corner of the Room, to show one another their Faces . . . for we are apt to write that in a

Letter to a Friend, which we would not have all the world know of, either our Concerns, or Inclinations.[25]

This view of letters as the means to secret information can be seen in quintessential form in the strain of epistolary fiction about spies: letters telling of plots, maneuvers, strange foreign customs, and even state secrets which have been uncovered, while the reader gets to spy on the spy.[26]

The revelatory possibilities of private letters were certainly promoted by publishers of epistolary fiction, who were at great pains to assure their audience that the letters being printed were from real people undergoing real stresses, and that the evidence had not been prepared for public eyes. Advertisements and Prefaces for letter novels tended to stress the authenticity and morality of the works: they could be valued as true life lessons. Dunton, in his publisher's preface to *The Post-Boy Rob'd of His Mail*, asked that he "undergo no censure for printing them as they came into my Hands, both regarding the Truth of Matter of Fact and exposing the [secret] Villanies of Mankind as they were. . . ." In addition, he asked his readers to send in any scandalous letters they might have lying around, for he said ". . . I believe there are few Men or Ladies who in their Lives have not met with some Intreagues or Occurances which may contribute to the Diversion of others. . . ." This insinuated the authenticity of the letters already in the collection and promised the public future volumes of letters from people just like themselves.

Billed as letters between friends, between lovers, collected from long journeys, and so on, these collections were often explained as turning up in deserted houses, in anonymous deliveries, or as being deliberately published by their owner to publicly heal a reputation, correct misinformation, or to give a wayward, heedless public the benefit of another person's experience. This tradition of letters goes back to Nicholas Breton's *A Poste with a Packet of Madde Letters* published early in the seventeenth century, which claimed that a postman happened "with a lack of heed, to let fall a packet of idle papers, the superscription whereof being only to him that finds it. . . ."[27] The pretence of realism is contradicted by the fact that the letters seem to come with their answers and that the whole is advertised as the first letter-writing manual in English. Later letter collections were more careful in their attempts at verisimilitude. The *Letters Writ by a Turkish Spy*, for instance, were "discovered, by meer chance in a corner of his Chamber, a great heap of papers; which seem'd more spoiled by Dust than Time."[28] To further authenticate the book, there is a glossary of Turkish words at the back of the volume to give assistance to those who do not understand all the words the Turkish spy used. The papers revealing *The Life of Marianne* were allegedly found in a similar way. The discoverer bought a country house and was making alteration in a cupboard in the wall, and "there was found a Manuscript of several Quires of Paper, containing the following History, all Writ in a Woman's Hand. . . . She gives herself the name of Marianne at the Beginning of her Narration."[29]

It seems a crude way to start: pawning off on the world a character who created herself in writing, a woman whose history is mysterious and who starts only as a nameless hand holding a pen. In fact all these novels which begin with the startled discovery of a heap of papers seem too literary and too obvious for our twentieth-century minds, used to more sophisticated tricks of realism. But according to at least one literary historian, readers in those days did believe that what they read was authentic:

The "common reader," living in an age of [modified] belief, did not find his credulity overstrained by a series of letters which told a story and which purported to be authentic, especially when elaborate devices to stimulate his suspension of disbelief were provided. He could hardly tell it from a collection of authentic letters unless he happened to move in circles where the facts were known.[30]

This may explain the avidity with which letter collections were bought and read.

The writers themselves contributed to this credulity by consistently denying charges of fabrication. Even with a book like *Robinson Crusoe*, Defoe insisted that it was all true. He wrote: "All the endeavors of envious people to reproach it with being a romance, to search it for errors in geography, inconsistency in the relation, and contradictions in fact, have proved abortive, and as impotent as malicious."[31] Eliza Haywood, whose tales of passion depended so little on belief for their effect, was always defending her veracity in her prefaces. "There are so many Things, meerly the effect of Invention, which have been published, of late, under the title of SECRET HISTORIES, that, to distinguish this," she insisted, "I am obliged to inform my Reader, that I have not inserted one Incident which was not related to me by a Person nearly concerned in the Family of the Unfortunate Gentleman. . . ."[32] The line she draws between fact and rumor is a tenuous one, but in 1729 such protestations were *de rigueur* because the public wanted stories that were true rather than invented. Similarly, one of the fictional letter writers in *The Polite Correspondence* makes a self-conscious claim for the "veracity" of her letters:

> If I have been troublesome to you by my long melancholy Letters I will now endeavor to make you some Amends. We have had strange Things happen'd in our Family, and had I the Pen of the Countess *d'Asnois*, or Madame *de Noyer*, I persuade myself my true History would not make a worse Figure than their feign'd ones. To you, however, a plain Detail of Facts will, I dare say, be more acceptable than any of those high finish'd Memoirs, wherein the Author's Ingenuity appears to much greater Advantage, than their Veracity.[33]

It is not by the events of her life, as compelling as those in any novel, that this character distinguishes her tale from the fictions she mentions. She claims the belief of her reader on the basis of the letter qualities of her prose. The first person style and the simple writing which lacks professional ingenuity are the evidences she uses to persuade the reader of her veracity. The distinction is an important one, for the letters included in earlier romances had always been written in the florid language of that tradition. When a heroine "blushed the Ruddy Morning open'd, the Rose-buds blew, and all the Pinks and Dazies spread, and when she sigh'd or breath'd, Arabia's Spices, driven by gentle winds, perfumed all around. . . ."[34] The characters who wrote such letters were not middle class, but fairy-tale kings and queens.

Indeed, the developing conventions of a realistic style gave an important advantage to letter fiction. At the same time that the manuals were recommending that letters "ought to favor of Carelessness, not so much different from our ordinary Manner of Speaking,"[35] and the prefaces to epistolary fiction were admiring the "Easiness of Stile and Address which is so beautiful in Writing of letters,"[36] the culture was settling into the conviction that the unvarnished truth could best be found in simple language and direct sentences. The unornamented prose style though appropriate to letters was simultaneously marked as the only mode suitable for writing or speaking the truth. By 1667, members of the Royal Society had insisted on "a close, naked, natural way of speaking" as a prerequisite to objective reporting. They preferred "positive expressions; clear senses, a native easiness; bringing all things as near as the Mathematical plainness, as They can; and preferring the language of Artisans, Countrymen and Merchants before that of Wits, or Scholars."[37] These emphases had an effect on prose style of non-scientific writing as well.[38] It was more important to write so that readers could understand the facts of a case than to display an author's education and wit.

These were qualities which came more easily to letter fiction than to other kinds of fiction. Margaret Cavendish advertised the charm of her *CCXI Sociable Letters* (1664) in the lack of "High Words" or "Mystical Expressions" and in the "Imitation of a Personal Visitation and Conversation,"[39] and Defoe congratulated himself for what amounts to "Mathematical plainness" in his preface to *A Continuation of Letters Writ by a Turkish Spy at Paris* (1718):

> Above all, I have followed that sure Rule In our Tongue, and which were it observed, would, I believe, be acknowledged to be the best Rule in all Tongues, (viz) to make the Language plain, artless and honest, suitable to the Story and in a Stile easie and free, with as few exotick Phrases and obsolete words as possible, that the meanest Reader may meet with no Difficulty in the Reading, and may have no Obstruction to his searching the History of things by their being obscurely represented.

Furthermore, it was claimed that women had a particular propensity for such unpretentious prose. Not only could they command the "easie Negligence of stile which is particularly required in Letters," and "Expression more from the Heart than from the Head," but it was felt that the subjects of letters were "natural to a Lady of good Fashion and a genteel Conversation to chuse. If we wanted a Proof that the Ladies excel the Men in Delicacies of this kind," claimed the preface to Mme. Du Noyer's *Letters from A Lady at Paris to a Lady at Avignon* (1716), "these Letters would be a very good one. . . ."

Although by modern standards, eighteenth-century letters seem rather formally composed, even then the conviction prevailed that letters were the spontaneous renderings of a person's innermost thoughts, especially in epistolary novels where letters were exchanged by confidantes or lovers. One thinks of the letters that Pamela wrote, for instance, as having been written quickly without hiding anything—seemingly written, as one of Richardson's fans remarked, "under the immediate impression of every circumstance which occasioned them, and that to those who had a Right to know the fair Writer's most secret thoughts.[40]

This "naturalness" of letters between intimates was especially emphasized in contrast to the classical or

exemplary letters in manuals. In his dedicatory epistle to
The Post-Boy Rob'd of His Mail (1692), Charles Gildon calls
attention to the difference between his candid collection
and the artificial letters in manuals:

> The difference betwixt *these Letters,* prompted by the several
> *immediate Occurances,* that occasion'd the writing of them, and
> those which some *Epistle-writers* have publish'd for Examples for
> the World to Copy after: *Nature,* and *Easiness* appear in the first;
> and *Study* and *awkard Pains* in the latter.

Another literary commentator put it this way:

> We write Letters to our Friends to let them know how Things are
> with us, and especially if they any Way relate to them, and we
> write every Thing we could say in case we happen'd to meet them.
> The Perfection of these Sorts of Letters consists then in their
> resembling common Discourse; that they be familiar and natural,
> and that they be not only free from the Umbrage of the Composi-
> tion, but that they surpass it, and that the Language of the Heart be
> felt in them. This is far from the Character of *Voiture's* Letters,
> instead of being natural, they are only witty, and imitate that Kind
> of Friendship that will not be imitated, they jest with it: This
> Writer feigns to feel what he does not feel. . . it seems that in him
> the Writer has devour'd the Man.[41]

Only "real" letters written frankly to friends would do—not
those written for effect. Voiture's more studied writing was
at odds with the new conventions in diction. Foreshadow-
ing the romantic idealization of spontaneity, it was felt that
true sentiment was incompatible with wit and the carefully
turned phrase.

Letters which expressed the "Language of the Heart"
rather than entertained or instructed in the old way were
preferred by the unevenly educated reading public who
did not enter easily into the spirit of elegant *bons mots* or
scholarly references. They could more easily sympathize
with the heroine of Marivaux's *The Life of Marianne,* who
preparing to tell the story of her life, asks herself "What
must an Author do to fall upon a stile? Is that of Books the

best? What then makes me dislike so much in most of them?" and decides "I will write this just as I would do a Letter,"[42] rejecting a more carefully planned style as artificial and even inauthentic. Her unalloyed humanity is further attested by the advertisement for the second part of these adventures, which claims that the writer is, "no Author, but only a Thinking Woman. . . ."[43]

Presumably such protestations enhanced a reader's estimation of a book since direct reporting of lived experience was more valued than the daydreams of some hack writer. *The Letters of Abelard and Héloise,* for example, begins with the boast that its contents are known to be real and therefore are to be preferred to the letters of the Portuguese Nun which might be composed:

> It is very surprising that the Letters of Abelard and Heloise have not sooner appeared in English, since it is generally allow'd by all who have seen them in other Languages that they are written with the greatest Passion of any in this kind which are Extant. And it is certain that the *Letters from a Nun to a Cavalier,* which have so long been known and admired among us are in all respects inferior to them. Whatever those were, these are known to be genuine Pieces. . . . These Letters therefore being truly written by the Persons themselves, whose Names they bear, and who were both remarkable for their Genius and Learning, as well as by a most extravagant Passion for each other, are everywhere full of Sentiments of the Heart, (which are not to be imitated in a feigned Story) and Touches of Nature, much more moving than any which could flow from the Pen of a Writer of Novels, or enter into the Imagination of any one who had not felt the like Emotions and Distresses.[44]

"Genuine" letters written with "Touches of Nature" were superior to those which were blatantly fictional because they were recognized as the results of living emotion, primary documents which demonstrated rather than described characters. And that is what, by their very nature, letters were best suited to do. Even within letter fiction, epistles were criticized if they seemed too literary, not sufficiently life-like. In *The British Recluse,* for instance, a disenchanted lover wrote to his frantic mistress that "The little Storms of Fury which appear in your letters, are too frequently met with in Stories to be wonder'd at. . . ."[45] The novelist even used her own literary banality in the service of "realism."

The line between the real and the fictional, deliberately blurred at that time by the purveyors of epistolary fiction, is at best a difficult line to draw distinctly. After all, there *were* two lovers named Abelard and Héloise who wrote letters to one another, but their letters, peddled to the public as just another tale of passion, are more or less indistinguishable from other sets of lovers' letters written as fiction. And who can say whether Alexander Pope's letters were real or fictional, written and sent as they were with an eye toward future publication? In his preface to those letters, Pope reports that booksellers on the lookout for letters promised rewards "to those who will help him to any," and goes so far as to say "Any domestick or servant, who can snatch a letter from your pocket or cabinet, is encouraged to that vile practice."[86] Presumably such purloined letters were printed; one does run across what appear to be real letters occasionally mixed in with collections of fictional ones, although both make use of the stock phrasing which plasters over individual differences anyway. One also assumes that some of the letters printed in real collections were written to fill out a volume. Nor is the issue of real letters itself easily untangled, for the writer hunched in his garret, putting words on paper, is as real a person as the correspondent sitting down to tell a story about an experience. Both choose a suitable stance from which to write, both compose from a mixture of memory and imagination.

The distinction between real and fictional letters also comes to feel pretty slippery when reading through the volumes of posthumously printed correspondence of real people, for these often read like fiction. It was an era in which people exchanged confidences and visited not by telephone or rapid transportation, but in full, careful, letters, and those letters that remain tell many a vivid story. For example, Lady Mary Wortley Montagu's youthful correspondence is very dramatic—that is, her sense of her life and the way she writes about her thoughts and experience is very dramatic. This is especially true of the series of letters written as she was preparing to run off with Wortley. (Many women carried on courtships in letters in order to circumvent disapproving parents or to preserve their reputations.) They are written with a sense of secrecy and danger, each one leaving the reader hanging in suspense in the best manner of a Richardson novel. In reading these letters it is hard to separate Lady Mary's real feelings from those engendered by the stress of the crisis times when she needed to communicate with Wortley. One cannot tell how much of her fearful urgency is a self-dramatizing of her secret relationship. Certainly having to conduct her relationship with Wortley in secret letters had its own separate effects on Lady Mary's emotions. Thus, although the difference between fictional epistolary novels and books of letters written by real people may have been meaningful to the reading public of that time, the distinction tells us more about the culture that read those letter books than it does about the books themselves.

It remains now to be shown how the letter collections, which fit so well the required stylistic conventions of the day, which appealed to the new audience of the literate middle class, and which the literary industry on Grub Street could turn out easily, led to longer epistolary fiction and to modern notions of the novel. One can point to certain tendencies toward coherence in these collections which have the effect when they are exaggerated, of transforming miscellanies into novels. There is, first of all, the compelling reality of a single persona behind a series of letters. Whenever a unique human voice can be heard in a collection of letters, it unifies the experience of the reader, who begins to develop a sense of the individual writing all the words. Another kind of unity is found in some of the extended exchanges in volumes of miscellaneous letters, in which the reader watches, and perhaps vicariously enjoys, the relationship between the two correspondents. Letter-writing manuals and books of instructive letters provided still another kind of coherent reading experience because they were didactic; and since their intention was to exhibit an exemplary consciousness for the reader to emulate, their success depended on creating believable ideals. Thus the authors of such books were earnestly trying to reach and affect their readers rather than simply pass the time with them, and the letters collected in a single volume have that common purpose. Each of these kinds of collections demanded the sustained imaginative effort of conjuring up the sort of persons who might write such letters, and so pulled the reader into the world of the book.

Not many of the letter collections published in the seventeenth century had these focused qualities. Most of them, harking back to Nicholas Breton's miscellaneous *A Poste with a Packet of Madde Letters* and to the endless variousness of the romances of the seventeenth century, set out to entertain and amaze their audience offering new tidbits of information and spinning new tales with new characters on every page. The letters in these collections provided no relationships to follow, no authorial purposes to understand, no characters for a reader to respond to or to care about—nothing, in short, to bind the reader's ever-changing experience. Not even the *Letters Writ by a Turkish Spy* (the first volume was published in 1687 and the complete eight volumes between 1691 and 1694), although presumably all written by the same person, build up any sense of a character. Travel books presented in letters, too, suffered from the uncontrolled diversity which prevented many early letter collections from passing into a novelistic mode. They did not include many personal anecdotes about travel or specific words to those back home; although they were crammed with information, there was no continuous sense of the person who sat down to write the letters. To a modern reader, reaping the seeds of empiricism sown in that century and surfeited with published facts and figures, volumes of travel letters like these can be pretty deadly.[47]

Before letters were fully exploited for their special qualities in telling stories, they were also pressed into service as the appropriate vehicle for gossiping in print about the great. Unfortunately, this was done in the simple-minded, name-dropping way of our modern scandal sheets, which grows very stale over the course of two centuries. Mme. D'Aulnoy's *The Present Court of Spain* (1693), for instance, chronicles the scandals and power plays in the court of Spain, where all purely political issues are thoroughly overwhelmed by love affairs and jealousies, and the political favors and decisions seem to be made almost entirely on the basis of these personal alliances. Similarly, Mrs. Manley's *Court Intrigues* (pirated separately in 1711, but first bound with Mme. D'Aulnoy's *Memoires On [sic] The Court of England* in 1695) are letters about the goings-on in different courts in Europe, with an occasional random, dull, personal letter to Mrs. Manley herself thrown in. The lack of connection among the letters makes the collection seem like a batch of documents printed as they were found, without any editing for coherence. Some appear to be spy reports, others reveal the private affairs of Europe's nobility. There are even some ostensibly written by dukes and princes, which show that even if an individual is rich and powerful, happiness is elusive. Indeed, love letters from monarchs read very much like love letters from poor citizens.

One reason that early fictional letters so often seem impersonal and flat to modern readers (when they are such an obvious device for developing complicated characters), is that the popular writers of light fiction were much more interested in thinking up clever plots than in working out the nuances of characters. This is apparent in Charles

Gildon's *The Post-Boy Rob'd of His Mail* (1692) in which one tantalizing situation after another is set forth with little sense of any of the characters. The framing story explains the collection as the contents of a mail pouch, stolen by a group of friends from one of the local coffee houses in order to publish and expose the vices and virtues of a random sample of people. All these fictional letters are interesting primarily for the gossip value of the situations they describe; "From a Servant, giving an account to his Mistress of all his Master's Failings in his absense from her"; "From a Debauchee, that had in mind to lead a penitent life"; "From a young Student, about an Apparition"; "From a young Lady to her Gallant, to whom she had yielded, and who was still Constant"; "From a morose Gentleman, exposing the Frailities of Woman." Each letter is followed by commentary—the conversation among the coffee house friends who by now are lodging for a few days in a house in the country, reading the letters aloud and discussing them. They judge each situation and rule on it with conventional wisdom, much as the courtiers of an earlier time posed chivalric dilemmas of love and honor to one another to while away the time.

These, then, were the popular early uses of fictional letters: travelogues, scandalous reports of the rich and powerful, and entertaining slivers of satire or bawdy comedy. But it is not among the abundant examples of these kinds of letters that the beginnings of the novel are to be found. For to succeed as fictional letters, such writing must be more than vehicles for wit or information. The novel-reader must be able to feel that the letters serve some more complicated function, such as release or clarification, for the fictional letter writer. They cannot be uniformly glib but must convey the sense that the writing is part of a complex interpersonal process that is not easy to set down accurately. Successful novels grew out of those fictional letters which took pains to delineate character (exemplary or otherwise) and sketched in a relationship between two or more people; it is to these we will now turn our attention.

Letters which imply an exchange, postulating a fictional correspondent at the receiving end and therefore appearing to have a true-to-life reason for being written in the first place, demand that the reader-at-home make an imaginative effort to intuit the relationship implied between the putative correspondents. Thus, reading becomes more than a passive act as it draws the reader-at-home into the world of the fiction, much as listening to one side of a telephone conversation invites a listener to project the meaning of the entire conversation. Reading a series of letters ought to be like entering into a relationship where an empathic effort is required to understand what is going on. As in watching mime, the audience must supply with the imagination what is missing from the stage.

It was Dunton, a publisher and writer famous for his sensational ideas (like his magazine of interviews with prostitutes)[48] who first recognized the appeal of letters which were written to seem like part of an exchange. In his autobiography he reported the moment of conception of his popular *Athenian Gazette*, an early version of Ann Landers, in which purportedly real letters from anonymous members of the public were printed along with responses from the editor. As he tells it, he was walking along with some friends one day when suddenly he stopped and cried out:

> Well, Sirs, I have a thought I will not exchange for fifty guineas; they smiled, and were very urgent with me to discover it, but they could not get it from me. The first rude hint of it, was no more than a confused idea of concealing the querist and answering his question.[49]

Dunton was right. This device of a personal letter to the editor caught the imagination of the public. In due time it was imitated by *The Spectator, The Tatler,* and *The*

Guardian, and to this day is a standard feature in many newspapers and magazines.

Love letters also proved to be popular with the reading public. They, too, imply an exchange, a relationship between two people, where infinite permutations were possible. In the miscellaneous collections there are epistolary rebuffs directed at overly importunate lovers, angry letters written to mistresses who have proved faithless, and scheming letters between lovers on how to manage a meeting. Many spin out the conventional lore about love affairs: that men tire rapidly of women who yield sexually, that money is more important than love in the success of a marriage, that women are especially susceptible to flattery and to jealousy. Others, supposedly reporting gossip to friends, relate an interesting anecdote: for example, the bawdy tale of a woman who blindfolds herself so as to be able to say she has not seen her lover, or of a man who dresses as a woman in order to gain access to his mistress. Eliza Haywood's *Love-Letters on All Occasions* (1730), for instance, included letters from men who have fallen in love with women, from women accusing men of designs on their chastity, long-winded letters between lovers about the fine points of emotion (i.e. distinguishing between tenderness and fondness), and so on.[50] There are charges and countercharges, declarations, proposals, acceptances, and refusals. All are about the pains and transports of love (which was Eliza Haywood's speciality), and they demonstrate how well letters were suited to expressing such emotions.

One of the longest sequences of such love letters to be included in a collection of miscellaneous letters—indeed, it is an epistolary novel in itself—is a correspondence between Theano and Elismonda appearing in Haywood's *Love-Letters.* The opening letter from Theano has the explanatory stage direction "On having obtained the last favor." Elismonda's guilt and remorse at having given in are gallantly answered by Theano's protestations of love. Then follow arrangements for rendezvous, some quick squabbles, and an enforced absence while Theano travels. That is the whole plot: nothing really happens except the ups and downs of the lovers' feelings and their uncertainties about one another. They write to each other constantly, even while in the same town and seeing each other. The letters build up in hysteria during an enforced separation towards a climax which follows in the wake of their correspondence. This climax, presumably a sexual embrace, occurs when the lovers are physically together, rather than writing letters; thus it does not take place on paper, but only in the mind of the reader-at-home. The last utterance in the story is "Hasten then to my fond longing Arms, for 'tis in the mute Rhetorick of Love that I can alone testify how passionately, how tenderly I am. . . ."[51] Thus the climactic events in this supremely verbal form are beyond words. It is one of the peculiarities of epistolary fiction that those events on which the story is centered always happen off-stage, so to speak, beyond the grip of words. Love-letters are always looking backward at earlier rendezvous or forward to longed for meetings, both of which are left up to the reader's imagination. These are the events which the characters relive and discuss in their letters to one another, because the epistolary structure dwells on responses to events rather than on the events themselves.

The other line of development from letter collections to novels goes through letter manuals. This can be seen in the complicated situations which authors invented in order to instruct their readers in morally correct responses to life. For although some of the letters in these manuals give helpful examples of epistolary etiquette for readers with the usual assortment of social problems, like gracefully declining a dinner invitation or writing a letter of condolence for some misfortune, for the most part the problematic situations depicted in these manuals were often not chosen for being typical. They were created by experts who were most interested in moral positions which required responses, preferring to set up complicated and unusual circumstances which tested the difficult cases. Farquhar's 1702 collection, for instance, has letters about how to rid oneself of cuckolds, how to importune a respectable lady for her attentions, as well as some discussing the advantages and disadvantages of marrying outside one's class. Sometimes the focus was a more mundane, but nevertheless difficult situation, such as how a parent might write morally compelling letters to a truant child or how a child might assert his independence without alienating his parents. Letter manuals, like the epistolary novels which followed them, often presented complex situations and then produced the tonally subtle and morally impeccable responses appropriate to them.

Occasionally the authors of manuals were carried away constructing awkward emotional situations in which there was more potential interest than in the conventional responses to them. In *A Compleat Academy of Complements* (1729), for instance, letters like "a forsaken maid's letter to her treacherous friend," or the one from "a beautiful young Virgin to rid a decrepit old man," are like the beginnings of novels, being realistic responses to dramatic situations. In Richardson's manual, *Letters Written To and For Particular Friends on the Most Important Occasions* (1741), there are also situations which go far beyond the usual occurrences of life. Although most of the letters in his collection are about proposing marriage, borrowing money, or the like, there is one from "A young woman in Town to her sister in the country, recounting her narrow Escape from a snare laid for her on her first Arrival by a wicked Procuress."[52] Another, written from "A Father to a Daughter in Service, on hearing of her Master's attempting her Virtue" was the first glimmering of *Pamela*, in which Richardson imagined this situation continuing for a time and followed through with responses to it.[53]

Manuals also foreshadowed novels in that they deliberately played with the subtleties of emotion. For example, in Richardson's collection there are three progressively less severe versions of a letter telling a young man that his romantic letter writing is too impertinent, and several examples of how to turn down a proposal depending on how much future encouragement the young lady wished to give. The possibilities inherent in the responses are emphasized with the subtle linguistic variations of each version. Unlike the entertaining fictional letters by Ward, Brown, or Gildon, who concocted their situations for comic effect, the letters in Richardson's manual are concerned with finding the right tones to embody different shades of sentiment.

Indeed, the letters in manuals were intentionally designed to train their readers' sensibilities in distinguishing among these shades of meaning. Thus, in a way, they were meant to take over the consciousness of their readers as the amusing vignettes in the miscellanies never could. The full title of Richardson's letter collection was "Letters Written To and For Particular Friends on the Most Important Occasions. Directing not only the Requisite Style and Forms To Be Observed in Writing FAMILIAR LETTERS; *But How to Think and Act* Justly and Prudently in the Common Concerns of Human Life." (italics mine). Such a book was not merely supposed to lay down rules of etiquette, but to educate for subtlety in one's moral relations to other human beings.

Certainly by Richardson's time, this had long been a recognized use of letter collections. As early as 1673, Hannah Wolley explained in her introduction to *The Gentlewoman's Companion* that she prepared herself for her secretarial task of writing letters for her mistress by reading others' sample letters not only to improve her writing, but to improve her sensibility:

There were not any who both wittily and wisely had publisht their

Epistles to view of the world, whom I had not read, and on all occasions did consult: those which I place in my greatest esteem were the Letters of Mr. Ford, Mr. Howel, Mr. Loveday, and Monsieur Voiture.[54]

She thought of her own volume of letters and other instructional devices similarly as a "compleat Directory" of living for "all of our Sex." In it she included sample dialogues between men and women in much the same spirit as she presents model letters—as examples, to her readers, of the properly sensible and delicate consciousness with which to live in the world. Her book is a collection of moral prescriptions for the maiden and the married: rules for everyday behavior (gait, gesture, speech), the good manners needed for dealing with those of a higher class, practical instruction in cookery, grooming, and household medicine.

Gentlemen also consulted letter manuals to sharpen discernment and refine the spirit. Dudley Ryder, a young man in the early eighteenth century, read model letters in order to acquire direction to his thinking as well as for pointers on style and social proprieties. For instance, this diary entry notes that he read Voiture's exemplary letters in order to set himself on the right mental track for letter writing:

Began to write to Aunt Stevenson. In order to do it read several letters of Voiture to help me fall into his way of thinking. I was extremely pleased with many of his thoughts.[55]

Letter manuals had this effect on their readers not only because each letter was intended to persuade the reader (either the fictive reader, the reader-at-home, or both) of some moral position, but because as a collection the didactic message was unified and consistent. Richardson sincerely identifies with the moral consciousness of the characters in his manual, for his letter writers are neither aristocrats nor rogues and whores. They are solidly middle class in their sentiments and attitudes, and these are the views consistently proselytized in the sample letters. There is one of "Advice from a Father to a young Beginner, what Company to chuse, and how to behave in it"; another is "From an Apprentice to his Master, begging for forgiveness for a great Misdeameanor"; a particularly stern one is written "to one who, upon a very short Acquaintance, and without any visible Merit, but Assurance, wants to borrow a Sum of Money."[56] They are all written in deadly earnest.

The development of such unified sensibility or point of view behind each collection, in which a certain way of reacting to life is prescribed however many different sets of circumstances are posed, is an important step in the direction of the novel. For at the most fundamental level, a novel temporarily usurps readers' minds allowing them to experience the world the way another consciousness would. The proselytizing manual consolidated just such a narrative stance, no matter how diverse the fictional authors of the letters.

The single consciousness, the serious moral intention which suffused the collections of exemplary letters, bound them together more tightly than the letters in miscellanies. This is the significant difference between epistolary fiction such as Richardson's, and light fictional letters such as Gildon's. In *The Post-Boy Rob'd of His Mail*, for instance, Gildon's satiric invention is behind each letter, creating caricatures for the amusement of the readers but not trying to reach them in any other way. To take a hypothetical case: if Richardson presented a letter from a father to a son against excessive drinking, it would be a genuine attempt to dissuade young men from drinking. It would be a persuasive, reasoned attempt to convince another, that audience of one. A letter on the same subject by Gildon, on the other hand, would be written with an eye towards entertaining the larger audience. He would make witty and clever sport of the gallant who tippled too much, rather than holding to the tone of a father trying to reach his son.

Because of Richardson's serious moral convictions, his letter exemplifying the way a father might try to convince his son not to be excessive would then reach beyond the putative recipient in fiction, to the audience of readers sitting at home. This is one of the most important ways in which Richardson's manual anticipates his novels.

Tracing change and growth is as much as can be accomplished by examining the collections of miscellaneous letters in circulation preceding the first appearance of full-fledged epistolary novels. Now it is time to speak more theoretically about letter fiction, tracing the effects of using letters to tell a story. The next two chapters form the core of literary theory about letters and fiction in this book, and perhaps will make clearer the ways in which fictional letters opened the door to the novel.

4

Separation and Isolation
in Epistolary Fiction

Epistolary fiction always works according to a formula: two or more people, separated by an obstruction which can take a number of forms, are forced to maintain their relationship through letters. This genre, which establishes such conditions just as arbitrarily as putting a knight on a plain, riding along in search of adventure, runs on the tension of one or both of these separated characters trying to surmount the obstacles between them in order to be finally united. Although some of these stories are about political intrigues in which the letter writers are spies or leaders of cabals plotting in secrecy, more often these epistolary tales are sexual intrigues, in which the main characters are thwarted lovers held apart by social or geographical distance. In either case, the characters are prevented from acting directly and can only respond to their difficulties by writing about them and hoping for a solution which will bring them together.

When played out in sexual terms, this standard plot aims at marriage or sexual intercourse between the separated hero and heroine. Inevitably their separation intensifies the lovers' consciousness of their longing for one another and their impatience for the marriage which is the end and proof of love in such novels, the salve for the persecution and loneliness which the characters invariably endure. Nor is this outcome a surprise, since the reader generally knows at the beginning whether or not the main characters will end up together. The stories are, in fact, more a matter of developing specific uncertainties and complications such as class differences, parental pressures, and certain moral prohibitions against sexuality, like prior marriages, incest taboos, or an insistence on chastity.

These are the standard barriers which keep lovers from their final intimacies and give rise to the sentiments expressed in the letters. Although the epistolary novel is pointed toward that blessed moment when all obstructions are eliminated and the characters can fall into each others' arms, the complications along the way create the novel by being the occasions for the characters' written feelings and thoughts. These complications are rarely significant in themselves; they simply furnish the reasons for the separation; the lives of the characters are presumed to have more scope than is shown in the particular episodes of the novel. What matters are the characters' responses to the roadblocks thrown up in their way, for these stories are about *reactions* to separation and isolation.

The letters which the characters write in response to their difficulties are the only means they have to cope with being kept apart, the only way they have to spend the energy summoned to deal with the frustration of their desires. Sometimes characters try to use their letters to plot their way out of their dilemmas, to manipulate the circumstances for their own ends. More often, however, writing is a more helpless response, a way of bewailing their plight, luxuriating in self-pity, detailing on paper and even enjoying the heightened awareness which comes from suffering. Thus, such stories told through letters have a built-in emphasis on the revelation and expression of personal feelings which are set before the reader in first-hand accounts. Even in third person narrations, descriptions of highly charged moments are bypassed with tactics like "it is more easily imagined than expressed" or "no description would do justice to the feeling" and sentimentalizing letters are brought forward to furnish the evidence for passion. For it is from letters that the reader gets a subjective sense of the characters and how they respond to their fates.

In dealing with frustration after frustration, the hero or heroine begins to be fixed in a characteristic mode of response which the reader can predict after a while, although it is tested by more and more extreme circumstances. The novel ends and the long-awaited dénouement is enacted only when this character-stabilizing process is finished. The epistolary novel makes use of external obstructions to motivate this process although later in the history of the novel, these obstructions became internal, psychological obstructions. In a Jane Austen novel, for instance, characters have to learn their private lessons, must change themselves, before they are rewarded with marriage. In epistolary novels, it is not the maturing of character which is presented, but rather the testing and defining of character, in an unpleasant sequence of pressing situations. Thus the final sexual contact between long separated characters can be seen not only as the novel's reward for those who have proven themselves to be persevering, faithful, and chaste, but also as a ringing down of the curtain on those who are unshakeably fixed in these virtues. It was one of the oversimplified conventions for women in these earliest novels that their sexual commitments sealed their fate, and that nothing beyond that needed to be settled to satisfy a reader's curiosity.

The other possible ending to epistolary novels is the death of one or more of the characters. These alternatives of sexual union or death make sense within the paradigm of the letter novel, for either one puts a stop to the letter writing and resolves the separation which the characters spend their fictional lives trying to overcome. Overt sexuality, presumably the object of the unfulfilled longings of the scribbling heroes and heroines, is the step which moves the main characters beyond the world of expressive sentiment which the novel of letters represents, and into some more self-contained state to which we readers are no longer privy. Death is a more extreme palliative. Where sex is the reward for those with fixed characters of the right sort, death is the just desert for those who are flawed—a solution which removes them from the stage just as effectively.

Any number of early epistolary novels demonstrate this formula. *The Unhappy Lovers* (1694), for example, of uncertain authorship, but thought to have been written by Mary Delariviere Manley, is about Mellecinda's ceaseless love and loyalty for her Artaxander despite the persecutions of her mother who wants her to marry the wealthy Lucidor. They are the conventionally perfect hero and heroine, unhappily separated because Mellecinda's mother hates Artaxander and covets the estate of his rival, Lucidor. The novel opens with a panegyric on the strength of LOVE, which it states can be proven by the "continual Inquietude that attends the most mutual Lovers, when absent but a moment . . . ," and the reader can be sure that the rest of the novel will develop all the particulars of "Inquietude." At first the wicked, scheming mother tries to force a marriage to the despicable Lucidor using an unsavory chaplain hired to say a few words over the unwilling girl. But this is just the beginning of poor Mellecinda's suffering, because when her mother cannot convince her to give up Artaxander, she resorts to more unscrupulous tactics. She fires Mellecinda's personal maid, the only person in the household Mellecinda can trust, and counterfeits an answer to one of Artaxander's letters, spinning a web of lies and misinformation around her daughter. Like Richardson's Clarissa, our heroine is soon sunk in a morass of deception that she cannot escape, with no one to turn to for help.

Mellecinda thinks ceaselessly of Artaxander for "Absence to Love is like oil to a greedy Flame, which makes it blaze up higher and burn more furiously."[1] As a balm to her pain and isolation, she begins to set her raving thoughts down in words—she "wou'd take an humour of writing on the Trees with her Diamond Bodkin, yet scarce knew what she writ." One day, having returned from his soldiering, Artaxander finds one of these bulletins and sees that she still loves him. He then initiates a secret correspondence with her, writing desperate love letters back and forth which they practically devour upon receiving: "He only fix'd his Eyes on the dear Name of Mellecinda as if he never would have done reading. He often Kiss'd it, though with so wild an Air, that you would have thought his Looks were now fierce and fiery, then soft and dying."[2] The lovers also manage other kinds of communication at a distance, and the reader lives through their tremulous response to a masque and a serenade. But after endlessly teasing each other and the audience with the ever-possible consummation of their love, Artaxander, alas, dies on the battlefield. We learn that at the very moment of his death, Mellecinda dreams that "she was dress'd up in a white veil." Somehow this book manages to use both death *and* marriage for endings. The last we hear of Mellecinda, she has entered a convent where "her thoughts are of Heaven, and to follow Artaxander."

In portraying the agonized responses of separated lovers to their fate, this novel holds out a hope of their eventual union until the very end, for each new proof of fidelity and suffering seems to demand this reward. And when neither Mellecinda nor Artaxander nor the reader can stand any more, the book ends, enshrining their persevering love and promising their union in the afterlife. The particular incidents of the plot are less important than the pervasive unhappiness and stoicism which their own letters to one another illustrate.

The Illegal Lovers: A True SECRET HISTORY being an

Amour Between a Person of Condition and his Sister
(1728), another anonymous epistolary tale which employs
the basic formula, establishes incest as the obstacle to the
novel's lovers. Bellario falls fatally in love with his wife's
sister when he brings his children to her to raise, obeying
his wife's deathbed wish. First he suffers silently, lament-
ing that "to call her Sister, which he once look'd on as a
Blessing, was in reality the extremest Curse of Fate,"[3] but
when she tries to discover from him the cause of his misery
he resorts to pen and paper for his distressing avowal. She
also replies by letter, upbraids him for his "criminal
Excess," refusing to have anything further to do with him.

Thus the stage is set; the episodes which follow are in
the best epistolary tradition of sexual brinksmanship, caus-
ing flurries of responses which fill out the rest of the novel.
First Bellario falls very ill, and the lady, who has also fallen
in love against all propriety, cannot stay away. While she is
visiting, passion overwhelms Bellario: "His eyes assum'd a
fiercer Blaze, his Cheeks grew red, his whole Frame
trembled with the inward Flame, he catch'd her in his
Arms, and pressing close her Lips with the most eager
burning Kisses, bore her to the Bed. . . ."[4] Fortunately for
our chaste heroine "a too great Impatience for Possession
depriv'd him of the Power,"[5] and once again the sexual
deed is left undone. Again the lady retires and Bellario can
only pursue her by mail. He writes her a letter in blood, a
proof of passion often found in these epistolary fictions,
and that temporarily convinces her to marry him. But she
vacillates her way through many more pages, in what is
supposed to be a dramatization of her conflict between
love and propriety, but what in fact is an interminable tease
for the reader. Even their neighbors discuss the lovers'
problem, debating whether or not it is moral for them to
marry. At last she agrees to let the church decide whether
or not they should marry. When this clerical verdict is
negative, Bellario, who has waited for so long, shoots
himself and the novel ends.

This novel, then, is also constructed out of the possibilities that the separated lovers may get to be together, a hope that is held out to the very end. The obstacle to their marriage is not strictly embedded in character (although the heroine's scruples prevent her from overturning convention), but lies in the accident of their legal connection. Their incestuous relation keeps them apart, writing unhappy letters to ease their pain long enough to make a story out of the situation.

As with many epistolary characters, association between these two is illicit. Mellecinda and Artaxander were forbidden to see each other by parental injunction; Bellario and his sister-in-law were prevented from marrying by custom, public opinion, and, finally, even the church. This was a favorite way to maneuver a plot into an epistolary format because it explained why people who wanted so badly to be in touch with one another would confine their relationship to letters. "Fly my Presence, as I for ever must do yours," writes an epistolary lover. "I am tyed up from every thing but Writing to you; that distant way of conveying to each other the meanings of our Souls is not forbid."[6]

Arranging a secret or difficult correspondence was more than just a convenient plot device; it was also a way to make the letters themselves the focus of the novel instead of functioning simply as the frame for the story. In epistolary fiction, narrative curiosity about the context and activity of the letters often adds a significant psychological component to the interest in the letters. For example, *The Fatal Amour Between a Beautiful Lady and a Young Nobleman* (1719) which is about an adulterous affair, is much improved by imagining different readers for the forbidden correspondence.[7] When the husband discovers the secret letters between his wife and the young nobleman, he mails them in a packet—along with his epistolary accusations to her and her written responses—to his wife's father with the request that his father-in-law chastise the wayward woman. This novel then becomes more than just another banal story of a cuckold because of its tangle of violated privacies: the husband was not supposed to read the letters between his wife and her lover, his wife certainly never meant her father to see them, nor her own damning replies about them to her husband. And none of it was intended for the eyes of the novel-reader, peering over the father's shoulder like an emotional voyeur. The fact that each set of letters is so charged, making their recipients so anxious, intensifies their interest for us.

Spy novels work like this, too, and epistolary fiction often ran to secret political machinations instead of secret sexual relations.[8] Notes written in elaborate codes and slipped surreptitiously into ambassadorial pouches, or assignations in the dark of the night, are bound to make correspondence more exciting than it is ordinarily likely to be. After all, when letters are contraband, and the very writing of them an illegal act, it gives luster even to the dullest of them.

Separating characters in epistolary fiction forces them to carry on their relationships in their imaginations, rather than act them out in their real lives. This accounts for the uncanny tenacity of epistolary relationships, because events in the imagination often have stronger hold on a person than do physical experiences in the material world. Everyday proof of this is in the difficulty we have dragging ourselves out of a good novel in order to attend to our "real" lives. After all, Mellecinda and Artaxander hardly spoke to one another during their long period of separation; yet their thoughts of one another sustained them through physical danger and the worst family hostility.

An incident from one of Scudéry's romances, described in *The Spectator*, images perfectly the way such epistolary relationships work:

> I remember in one of *Scudery's* Romances, a couple of honourable Lovers agreed at their Parting to set aside one half Hour in the Day to think of each other during a tedious Absence. The Romance tells us, that they both of them punctually observed the time thus

agreed upon; and that whatever Company or Business they were
engaged in, they left it abruptly as soon as the clock warned them
to retire. The Romance further adds, That the Lovers expected the
Return of this stated Hour with as much Impatience, as if it had
been a real Assignation, and enjoy'd an imaginary Happiness,
almost as pleasing to them as what they would have found from a
real Meeting.[9]

The speaker here is not interested in his example as an
exploration of the potency of consciousness but as an
after-dinner joke, introducing it facetiously as an "Expedi-
ent for the Alleviation of Absence." But he misses what a
telling example it is of the workings of romantic love, not to
mention epistolary relationships, this tale of lovers who
experience a kind of vicarious love in their imaginations.
His lovers can summon up images of each other, without
need for the visible presence of the other, and then react
joyfully to their own creations. Just so, love is available
even when lovers are not, in the solitary pleasures of
reading and writing love letters.

The degree to which love letters are treated symbolically
can be judged from the way epistolary characters behave
with these poor, inanimate, pieces of paper. In virtually
every epistolary novel, letters are kissed, embraced, moon-
ed over, communed with, treasured—as if they were stand-
ins for the absent lover. Mrs. Manley begins one of the
letters in *Court Intrigues* with this flaming avowal: "Your
Letter was my Bedfellow last Night; I laid it upon my
Breast where my Heart beat it a Thousand wel-
comes...."[10] One of Farquhar's *Letters of Love and
Business* ends by assuring its object that the writer was
about "to see her in a lively Dream, since the last thing I do
is to kiss her dear Letter, clasp her charming Idea in my
Arms, and so fall fast asleep."[11] Another epistolary lover
tells his correspondent: "I flung myself down on the couch
and hug'd the divine Paper, and Kiss'd the Superscription
for above an hour and then open'd it...."[12]
The letter writer fantasizes the beloved and writes to that

shadow; the letter reader conjures up the beloved writer in order to savor the words fully. The heroine in *Love-Letters Between A Nobleman and His Sister* explains that she takes pleasure in penning her thoughts to her beloved because the writing itself seems to link her to him. "For while I write, methinks I am talking to thee; I tell thee thus my Soul, while thou, methinks are all the while smiling and listening by; this is much easier than silent Thought, and my Soul is never weary of this Converse. . . ."[13] Other characters similarly noted that writing put them in the beloved's presence, an hallucination often relished in the letter itself:

> I have at this Moment so lively an *Idea* of you, that I almost fancy you here in Person. Methinks how very kind you are! How affectionately you condole me for the Torments I have suffer'd in your Absence; and how Thankful I am to you for them! How you press my Hand, and swear you will never part with me![14]

As in the Scudéry romance, faithful lovers could set aside each day at least the amount of time needed to write a letter, and spend those hours creating the image of the loved one and then writing to that creation.

These images of absent lovers are, of course, the writers' own projections and can have little or nothing to do with the other correspondent. *Five Love-Letters From a Nun to a Cavalier*, the so-called Portuguese Letters, are an entirely one-sided correspondence in which the Portuguese nun, Marianne, entreats, upbraids, and verbally caresses the French soldier who first seduced her, made her love him, and then left her. Since no response comes from him, her letters, in order to sustain themselves, imagine him and fabricate *his* responses. She complains about his indifference, imagines his rebuke, and asks pardon. She plays both parts, providing for herself the cavalier's possible responses and then answering them.[15] This sort of internal conversation is commonly found in the letters which characters write one another in the early novels and is the inevitable result of long-distance communication.

A more modern example of the use of a letter as a place where one can invent a version of the other person's thoughts in order to answer them is Franz Kafka's *Letter to His Father*. In this extraordinarily bitter essay, he addresses his father and delivers to him all of the resentment gathered from childish memories and mature introspection. Although many people surely have had fantasies about such a letter, in which they finally say everything they have always wanted to say to their parent, the level of energy and detail in Kafka's letter immediately strikes the reader as unusual. It seems to be a relationship that fills his moments with the vividness of fantasy. Indeed, he is the first to admit that brooding about his father generated most of his early writing: it is a relationship he has carried about in his head for a long time. He writes to his father as if to an implacable wall, with no compassion or human fellow-feeling. In order to justify what he is putting down on paper he must conjure up a terrible monster as the receiver of his indictment. He is not interested in a real response to his letter from the other person to whom it is addressed. He is interested in setting down in black and white, as a kind of exorcism, all the harshest truths he can bear about himself and how he got to be the way he is.

When he is finished, he assumes his father's voice in order to answer his own bitter recriminations. It is as if his father is always available to him as a role he can call upon whenever he wants to. He puts words into his father's mouth to counter his long accusation, words in which his father defends himself with the charge that Kafka has exaggerated the father's vileness in order to excuse the son's shortcomings. He then puts on his own hat again in the imagined dialogue and responds to the counterfeited rebuttal with a deep awareness of the game he is playing:

My answer to this is that, after all, this whole rejoinder—which can partly also be turned against you—does not come from you, but from me. Not even your mistrust of others is as great as my self-mistrust, which you have bred in me. I do not deny a certain justification for this rejoinder, which in itself contributes new material to the characterization of our relationship.[16]

Kafka knows that his letter is the medium for a complex evolution of two voices. The father Kafka imagines, and to whom he is writing, is made up by Kafka. To draw out his real feelings of anger and frustration, he must first create a caricature of his father, then confront it, head on. Like an anti-Pygmalian, he hates what he creates. And the alternation between believing his creation and recognizing its factitiousness is stunning.

Thus, letters are a particularly potent medium for fantasy because they have the magical ability to bring people to life; addressing others on paper evokes their palpable presence. For Dona Teresa, a character in a novel by Mrs. Manley, writing to her lover becomes an addictive form of fantasy. Because only when writing can she drift into the emotional wash of love she craves, all other activities are subordinated to it; her correspondence is the thing that matters most in her life. She writes at all times of night or day, whenever she can find the privacy and solitude to do it:

'Tis now Three in the Morning, and I have been thinking of nothing but Means to write to you. As soon as I found my Mother was fast asleep, I got up, and for want of other Paper, which is a Commodity prohibited in my Apartment, I tore out the white leaves of a Book, to enable me by that means to let you know with how much Pleasure I sacrifice to you the Moments I can rob of my Repose. I only know the Nights by the Liberty they afford me of writing and thinking of you. While other people are asleep, Love and My Misfortunes keep me awake. I think of the Minutes I have pass'd with you, of the Difficulties which now deprive me of the like Happiness. . . .[17]

The impediments to her continued relationship, the prohibitions of her mother, only make Dona Teresa more determined to hold onto the thread of epistolary connection with her lover. Balked by her circumstances, writing becomes the only way to triumph over her difficulty, not only because of the pleasure of disobedience, but because it renders something out of her suffering.

In other words, the problem of lovers in epistolary novels is a kind of writer's problem: the world makes sense only as they write about it. The writing gives meaning to living, not the other way around. Occasionally this living-in-writing gets carried to ridiculous extremes, as when Sylvia in *Love-Letters Between A Nobleman and His Sister* laments:

> Oh *Philander*, it is two tedious Hours Love has counted since you writ to me, yet are but a quarter of a Mile distant; what have you been doing all that live-long while? Are you not unkind? Does not Sylvia lie neglected in your thoughts?[18]

Absurd as it is, this complaint is intended seriously and shows the degree to which letters *were* the relationship between two such epistolary lovers. Letters claimed the undivided attention of the other for at least as long as it took to read and think about the letter. As a character from *Love in Excess* put it: ". . . when I can neither see you, nor hear from you, to write, gives some little respite to my Pains, because I am sure of being in your Thoughts while you are Reading my Letters."[19]

In one of the "Portuguese Letters," the letter-writing nun is so involved in writing her letter that she will not relinquish it, fairly tussling over it with the man who is supposed to deliver it for her. The fantasy world in which she communes with her absent lover is very precious to her, and she knows her imagination holds her in it as long as she is writing. That is far more important to her than communicating a particular message by mail. She writes:

> The officer that waits for this Letter grows a little Impatient: I had once resolv'd to keep it clear from any possibility of giving you

Offence. But it is broken out into Extravagances, and 'tis time to put an end to 't. But Alas! I have not the heart to give it over. When I write to you, me-thinks I speak to you: and our Letters bring us nearer together. . . . The Officer calls upon me now the fourth time for my Letter. He will go away without it, he Says; and presses me, as if he were running away from another Mistress. Farewell. You had not half the difficulty to leave me (tho' perhaps for ever) which I have, only to part with this Letter. But Adieu.[20]

She hangs onto her writing, for that is where the relationship is. The written word does not merely express her connection to her far-away cavalier, it brings it into being.

In this literary genre, writing was a plausible enough response to separation and aloneness so that epistolary characters turned to letter-writing in unhappy times as their only alternative to direct action. From Mellecinda who went raving through the woods writing on trees (rather like Orlando in *As You Like it*) and Bellario who kept importuning his sister-in-law to marry him, even to the point of writing with his own blood, or Dona Teresa creeping about silently at three in the morning in order to pen her repetitious sentiments to her lover, to the Portuguese Nun who would rather write her passionate letters than mail them, these characters wrote to reflect on themselves and their circumstances, not to change them. The letter to Kafka's father never got sent, finally; its purpose was not simply to confront his father but to formally externalize his own thoughts. The famous letters that Héloise and Abelard wrote to each other were written in remembrance and meditation after they were already separated for life. The Portuguese Nun's letters, too, were written after her love affair had come to an insurmountable impasse. Even those letters written by Pamela were not expected to affect the circumstances which threatened her, but were meant to be shared with her distant parents.

But to create epistolary fiction, an author had to arrange more than the separation of two people who loved and depended on one another. Some provision had to be made to isolate the individual from all others as well. Again and again these books return to the scene of a character shut up alone in a room with some paper and a pen. It is a middle-class image, of course, because it takes money to provide such rooms, and a fairly high degree of literacy for the temptations of pen and paper to mean anything. Probably, too, the degree to which the solitude was portrayed as unnatural and trying, weighing heavily on the persecuted characters, reflected the cultural ambivalence about the relatively new emphasis on privacy and individualism. But while this basic epistolary situation spoke to the condition of its particular middle-class, urban audience, the locked door and the writing implements were also just a new set of props for the old, familiar Puritan formulation of the way in which an individual—like Robinson Crusoe on his lonely isle—must wrestle in privacy and solitude with the imagination.

Since these characters are often women, being locked in their rooms also dramatizes their alienation from a society which denied them their political and economic rights. But at the most basic level it speaks to the deeper truth that people are locked in their own skins, in their own consciousnesses, a circumstance which generates the curiosity about other people that novels set about to satisfy in the first place. An implicit assumption of human isolation pervades these novels for which the solitary situation is a metaphor. When crucial letters are hopelessly misdirected, or false ones forged by villains, the ensuing misunderstandings somehow typify the difficulties inherent in all human communication.

Sometimes this isolation is emphasized by using characters who are symbolically separated from the rest of society: nuns or convicts or world-weary hermits secluded in some pastoral refuge. Sometimes too the isolation is more moral or psychological than physical and the protagonists are pictured as people perpetually exiled, living in the midst of those who refuse to understand them. Such is the miserable lot of the heroines of *The Unhappy Lovers* (1694), *The Rash Resolve* (1724) and the more familiar *Clarissa* (1748)—all of them prisoners of hard-hearted parents or guardians determined to bring their recalcitrant daughters around to marriages they do not want.

Because loneliness is a condition of consciousness, dwelling upon it in writing can only intensify a morbid awareness of it. The letters written by the Portuguese Nun alone in her convent cell, for instance, are violently longing as direct speech would never have been. This makes epistolary characters more susceptible to the manipulations, whether cruel or kind, of others. Their dependency upon the insufficient and uncertain methods of eighteenth-century mail deliveries also emphasizes their helplessness, particularly when caught in hostile circumstances. The fact that a Pamela or a Clarissa is at someone else's mercy is underscored because the reader learns of it at a great distance in a letter.

The inevitable time lag of long-distance communication caused misunderstandings to continue at great length, bringing many complications in their train. It often required an extended correspondence to unravel snarls which could have been quickly cut in a few minutes of direct conversation. Operating ironically, however, the author permits the reader to have access to all the letters while the characters themselves are often ignorant of some crucial fact, thereby deepening the sense of their isolation for the reader. In a tale by D'Urfey, for instance, a husband discovers a note from his wife to a handsome monk, and insinuates himself into the correspondence, slowly hatching a plot which will punish her for her adulterous passion. The reader, who knows the whole story, watches it grind out inexorably, feeling as helpless as the victim in the fiction.[21]

Although some characters are forced into their rooms to write their letters through the evil offices of others, some are separated for less dramatic reasons of social alienation common enough among us all. The heroine of a novel called *The Polite Correspondence* is separated from her father, for instance, because she is younger and from a generation more modern than his; she chooses to write a letter to him rather than to speak to him, although they live in the same house. (Indeed, he reads it in her presence.) The advantage for the character is that she insures an exact wording of her message, leaving nothing to the chances of spontaneous conversation. The advantage to the author is that it allows an exact copy of this letter to be sent off to the distant lover when he is told about the episode, and so is a device which gives the reader a full set of documents.

In other stories, a constraining sense of respectability inhibits free talk among the characters and drives one or another to a private room to write out statements for others to read. Bellario in *The Illegal Lovers*, it will be remembered, confesses his love to his sister-in-law in writing, in deference to the impropriety of their situation. Eliza Haywood was always creating characters in her epistolary fiction whose natural delicacy of feeling forced them to resort to writing rather than to direct speech. In *Memoirs of a Certain Island* (1725) she portrays a man who counterfeits shyness and modest respect for a sensitive woman by declaring his attraction to her in writing, rather than in person. Two women who meet at a country inn in *The British Recluse* (1722) although curious about each other's lives, are restrained by decorum from telling each other their stories face to face. But they hit upon the charming solution of enlightening one another by letter, and each goes off to her room to pen her autobiography for the other—and us—to read. Similarly, in *Love in Excess* (1719), Haywood allows the hero, a married man who must not be seen too often with his beautiful young ward, to both maintain his respectable façade and to circumvent convention, by writing the secrets of his heart in letters to her.

Emotional self-description comes easily to letters, because one can better recognize and confess to the power of feelings when alone and unhurried. But then the rhythm of these feelings, as they build and subside, becomes the subject of the letters. When Héloise sat down to write out and relive the history of her relationship with Abelard, she was not doing it to inform Abelard of what happened, for he had been there too. Nor was she trying to convince him of anything with her remembered tale. She was recapitulating her own emotional history, right up to the present moment when, as she reports, "there rises unexpectedly from the Bottom of my Heart a passion which triumphs over all these notions [i.e. her nun's vows of chastity]."[22]

The letters of the Portuguese Nun, the earliest and one of the best examples of epistolary fiction, are a fine illustration of this self-contained process. The nun writes to her soldier-lover of her love for him, and her bitterness because he left her and does not even answer her letters. She writes herself in and out of her passion, for which words are both a catalyst and a record. At first she lengthily and dramatically beseeches him to return to her or at least to respond to her passionate avowals. Later her feeling turns to condemnation of his impervious silence. Within each letter she goes through many stages of emotional fervor, riding her own waves. By the end of the series of five letters, she has decided to try to forget him and write no more. The reader sees her trying to hold onto her sensations, trying to work herself into believing in that love. But finally when she stops sustaining and energetically pushing it, the whole apparatus falls of its own weight and the affair is over.

Throughout the "correspondence," the Portuguese Nun mistakes her own emotional energy for a two-way affair. When she dismisses the officer who comes to pick up her letter, and pens yet another line to her "lover" telling him she is going to start a new letter, she embodies the solitary letter-writer, sitting alone, writing letters to no one but herself. *"The Officer will be gone,"* she writes. "Well and what matters it? Let him go. 'Tis not so much for your sake that I write as my own; for my Business is only to divert, and entertain myself. . . ."[23] Finally she has come to understand that she is writing for herself and not for him. The act of writing itself, her imaginings of the affair and her own consciousness have become more important to her than the man who is presumably to receive her letters.

An odd sequel to this little novel, written by another hand to cash in on the success of the "Portuguese Letters" shortly after they were translated and available in English, is a set of letters claiming to be the cavalier's missing responses. Nor can this newer cavalier forbear from commenting on the obvious one-sidedness, the blankness towards the other, the self-involvedness, which is so remarkable in the nun's letters. "But to what end do you write so often to me, since my Answers never come at you?" asks the cavalier, assuring her of his devotion, anxious that his letters are not getting through. This sequel perverts the original tale—the tragedy has not been of a false lover but of a failure in communication—and emphasizes how the nun kept writing even when her letters never reached their destination. The cavalier promises to do the same: "I will continue writing to you" he says like a proper epistolary character who lives only for his writing, "for I am never better satisfied, nor do I breath with so much ease at any time as when I have a Pen in hand to write to you; but I become heartless and miserable and seem ready to die as soon as I lay it aside."[24]

Nor is this example unique. All through letter fiction there are references to the self-directedness of the writing. In Thomas Brown's *The Adventures of Lindamira*, for instance, the hero Cleomidon, separated from Lindamira for most of the story, confesses to her at the end that for many years he wrote and then destroyed love letters whose only audience was himself. During the long, melancholy years of marriage to a woman he did not love, he consoled himself with his feelings for his true love—Lindamira:

> I took those opportunities of being in my Closet; and, to confess
> the truth, I spent much time in thinking on you and writing to you:
> I complain'd of the rigor of my Fate; I demanded your Advice in a
> thousand little Occurances; I sent my wishes for your Happiness
> and for a sight of you, ten thousand more; but, after all, I durst not
> disobey you. I burnt my Letters, then wrote again; then sacrific'd
> them to the flames; and in this manner did I pass my days.[25]

There was no audience for these letters but an imagined
mistress and himself, and yet he wrote them continually.
Their purpose was not to communicate anything but to
slake some psychological thirst for externalized consciousness. The words are not there to inform anybody else of
anything; they are simply the only way of dealing with an
insoluble problem.

The fact that this way of coping with unhappiness does
not change anything explains in large part why epistolary
fiction is usually so repetitive. In later fiction these effects
are often modulated by varying the detail of the occasions
for these repetitive responses, but the early novelists
seemed content to let the compulsive writing of their main
characters stand undiluted. There is a certain amount of
human truth in this repetitiousness of course; unhappy
people do cover the same ground over and over. "Methinks
I run over and over too often with the story of my own
deplorable condtion. . . ,"[26] the Portuguese Nun notices.
Suffering brings consciousness in its wake, the consciousness of self, of psychological process, and although writing
relieves the suffering somewhat, it also insists upon a
simultaneous awareness of the pain. In her last love letter
to the cavalier, when the Portuguese Nun realizes how sick
her obsession has finally become, she writes:

> But I will never have any more to do with you. I am a fool for
> saying the Same things over, and over again so often. I must leave
> you, and not so much as think of you. Now do I begin to Phansie
> that I shall not write to you again for all This; for what Necessity is
> there that I must be telling you at every turn how my Pulse
> beats?[27]

She recognizes that she has not been recording every pulse beat for his benefit. Rather, she writes out the impossibility of the exercise of any other power.

Of course, there are other reasons for engaging in the process of letter-writing besides the need to write oneself out of a certain obsession. Any individual who has had the time for an extended correspondence knows how agreeable it is to settle back to investigate his or her impressions more fully, to indulge in the desire to write them to a sympathetic ear. In this state of heightened consciousness, there are pleasures of intense awareness.

Soren Kierkegaard, a nineteenth-century philosopher who interested himself in questions of consciousness, chose an epistolary format to tell the story of a poet who wanted to keep alive a heightened, romantic sense of himself, because it was the artistic persona from which he wrote. A habitual letter-writer, he did not care if there were answers to his letters or not.[28] He also carried on a romance at some distance, keeping it teetering on the brink of consummation as long as possible, because he preferred to think about it rather than enact it, in order to preserve it as a subject for poetry. He even withdraws from the relationship, disappearing without a trace, in order to keep reality from intruding on the vision of romantic love which so inspires him. And all the time, of course, he writes self-conscious letters about his choice to his friend.

"My love cannot express itself in marriage" writes the poet to the narrator of the tale. "The very instant reality comes into question, all is lost, it is then too late."[29] He wants to indulge himself in his feelings about his love without having to have a real relationship with her. Like the Portuguese Nun who lives in her own writings about love, or Goethe's Werther who falls in love with a woman he knows is unattainable and then "enjoys" the intoxication of his own emotions in letters to a friend, so too is this lover-poet in love with his own consciousness of love. Kierkegaard explains that the poet's refusal either to give up his love or to consummate it is a way of protecting the creative energies that the feelings of love generate. Love liberated the poet in the young man, but he must leave his lady if he is to preserve that part of him which has turned poet.

It makes sense that in this parable of love and poetry, feeling and writing, the character who is reluctant to enter a daily "marriage" to another chooses letters as his form of personal contact. Letters allow a person to keep a relationship going in the imagination, away from tarnishing actuality. The poet-lover of this tale is shrewd in knowing the value of what he already has and in fearing the effects of consummation. He prizes his own sensibility and writing about it more than the woman herself and does not want to confront his inner experience with the actual woman. As Kierkegaard points out, his letters about her are really about his own self-awareness:

> So again the girl is not a reality but a reflection of the movements within him and their exciting cause. The girl has a prodigious importance, he actually will never be able to forget her, but what gives her importance is not herself but her relation to him. She is as it were the boundary of his being.[30]

The girl herself is almost irrelevant, like the Portuguese Nun's cavalier. Each is merely the accidental cause of the emotion which is the real introspective focus of the letters.

Because so many epistolary fictions are about subjective realities—and what else could they be about, consisting as they do of the outpourings of lavish consciousness heightened by suffering and by isolation—they always end (or essentially end) when those unsettling subjectivities are laid to rest, when those forces which keep the book in motion are satisfied. Therefore, the tension in any epistolary novel is built up out of the antagonism of two states of mind: the pull of consciousness and oblivion or at least quiescence. The characters try to transcend their

problems; the subjective consciousness is always struggling to objectify itself. Abelard writes,

> I was born with violent Passions; I daily strive with the most
> tender Emotions, and glory in triumphing and Subjecting them to
> Reason.[31]

He is trying to transmute his private sentiments into public
feelings, his personal passion into impersonal grace. He
writes to Héloise and tells her of his tortured wrestlings
with himself:

> What means have I not used? I have armed my own Hands against
> myself; I have exhausted my strength in constant Exercises; I
> comment upon St. Paul; I dispute with Aristotle.... How can I
> separate from the Person I love, the Passion I must detest? Will
> the tears I shed be sufficient to render it odious to me? I know now
> how it happens, there is always a Pleasure in weeping for a
> beloved Object.[32]

Abelard keeps trying to deal with himself, attempting to
make himself behave. But if he solves his problem and rids
himself of his detested passion, it will no longer be
necessary to write, as it is no longer necessary to scratch
when an itch is gone.

This is something which the Portuguese Nun does not
understand when she pens her last love letter to her
cavalier. Without realizing that it is her very discomfort
which impels her letters, she makes this naive prediction:

> Within a While, you may yet perhaps receive another Letter from
> me, to shew you that I have outliv'd all your Outrages, and
> Philosophiz'd myself into a state of Repose. Oh what a Pleasure it
> will be to me, when I shall be able to tell you of Your Ingratitude,
> and Treacheries without being any longer Concern'd at them my
> Self![33]

But, of course, that calm and collected letter never gets
written. The impulse for writing the sort of letters which

comprise a fiction comes from the need to write in order to cope with a situation in which action is desired but not possible. One writes in order to *become* calm and collected; when that state is reached there is no longer any need to write. Sometimes the agonized individual consciousness resolves itself by being converted into some kind of public-mindedness. Fictional nuns either marry or die or, as in the case of Abelard and Héloise, they surrender to a communal, monastic, disciplined Catholicism which has no room in it for individualized sexuality or romantic love. Marriage can also be a way of transcending the privacy of self in these novels, because two people face any difficulty together. Marriage is too public and too social a state to permit the kind of solitary thrashing about which makes up the story of an epistolary novel.[34] But it works as the perfect ending for such a book because it resolves the subjectivities into objective facts—love into a contract, individual awareness into a social consciousness—and so dissolves the very things which have kept the plot going.

In fact, isolation is so central to the epistolary paradigm that if the plot solves it, with a marriage for instance, before the novel is finished, it continues in an entirely new form. Instead of beng an exploration of heightened consciousness, the book then becomes a public disquisition on social concerns. The classic instance of this is Pamela, which stops being about the consciousness of Pamela once she is actually married to Mr. B., and turns into a tract on class differences. No longer is Pamela's virtue tested; instead it is the familiarity with the roles of her new class, scrutinized by her new adversary, her sister-in-law the fault-finding Lady Danvers. Nor does Mr. B. continue as a *provocateur* for Pamela's letters home; his new function is to provide the information for her (and all the little Pamelas in the reading audience) on how to act like gentry, how to behave when suddenly called upon to change class or station overnight.

But other epistolary novels, too, use this strategy when they move away fom examining the individual consciousness of characters. Once the seduction is accomplished in *Love-Letters Between A Nobleman and His Sister*, for instance, it centers on the larger social question of the limits of legality within a constituted society. Similarly, *Les Liaisons dangereuses* is concerned with retribution and paying one's moral debts and *La Nouvelle Héloise* turns into a master plan for utopian living, once their respective heroines are no longer in a solitary, embattled, state.

The isolation of the characters is essential to the epistolary formula because it throws the characters back into themselves, to probe their own thoughts, their own feelings. Their separation from others inevitably magnifies their reactions, makes them vulnerable and suggestible, and provides a steady flow of responses to record. What the characters enact in their seclusion is at the core epistolary novel: a self-conscious and self-perpetuating process of emotional self-examination which gathers momentum and ultimately becomes more important than communicating with anyone outside the room in which one sits alone writing letters. So the isolation is finally complete, whether it was begun by accident, as a result of social decorums, or as an inhumane punishment; and it continues until the outside world intervenes with some natural force—like sex or like death—to neutralize it.

5

The Self As Word in Epistolary Fiction

It seems natural to us by now to think that what a novel does is examine the consciousness of one or more characters: to re-create the inner atmosphere of their minds, to note their predispositions to see the world in a particular way, and to record how the blessings and torments of their lives rearrange these predispositions in the course of time. But it is because of the epistolary form that this has become the pattern for a novel, for unfolding a story in letters automatically emphasizes the psychological angle of vision as no other narrative form does. Because the letter-writer's imagination is involved in the translation of experience into language, a fiction told through letters becomes a story about events in consciousness, whatever else it may be about.

These novels are also inherently self-reflexive, automatically about themselves as instances of written experience. Romances never played with these boxes within boxes, the levels of reality established in epistolary novels. There were no letter-reading characters to direct the novel-reader back to himself, no writers to mirror the activity of their authors. This suggestive confusion about subjective experience as one person writes it and someone else reads it is another distinguishing characteristic of the modern novel, because it extends the meaning of the fiction past its plot to explore the way human beings self-consciously sift their experience, transform evanescent perceptions into personal meanings, and construct their interior realities.

One effect of telling stories about the consciousness of the characters is that it gives a continuous sense of time even where there is no formal unity of time or place in this genre. The reader soon disregards the formal dislocations and paces himself instead to the inward rhythms of the epistolary characters who are always reacting to the present. The immediacy of such writing also encourages the inclusion of all the psychological particulars. For when the writer is recounting something from the past, as in a memoir, knowledge of the outcome influences the telling, pruning much of the surrounding detail. However, when writing about an event while living through it, all the immaterial psychological nuance seems potentially relevant and deserving of attention.

Memoirs are tidier than epistolary novels because there are no false starts, no loose threads. They shape, with hindsight, the pattern of life's miscellaneous happenings. Epistolary novels, on the other hand, show minds interpreting events as they happen, blind to future consequences, encouraging the reader to live through them as well. This is what Samuel Johnson meant when he told Thomas Erskine that "if you were to read Richardson for the story, your impatience would be so much fretted that you would hang yourself. But you must read him for the sentiment, and consider the story as only giving occasion to the sentiment."[1] Richardson himself, introducing *Sir Charles Grandison*, wrote:

> The Nature of Familiar Letters, written, as it were, to the *Moment*, while the Heart is agitated by Hopes and Fears, on Events undecided, must plead an Excuse for the Bulk of a Collection of this Kind. Mere Facts and Characters might be comprised in a much smaller Compass: But would they be equally interesting?[2]

A book like Crébillon's *Letters From the Marchioness de M*** To the Count de R****, which has no active plot to speak of, "paint[s] in the warmest Colours, the Progress of an unfortunate Passion, from its seducing Birth to its fatal Period; and represent[s] an amiable Mind variously agitated by the Impressions of Tenderness, and the Dictates of Duty."[3] The Marchioness' letters, written day by day to her lover, invite the reader to watch a mind reveal itself as she agonizes over the same things again and again: she is afraid the Count's indiscretion will give her away; she resolves never to see him again; she relents and hotly summons him:

> The pensive Air which my Husband assumed yesterday, alarm'd me not a little; I was apprehensive, that you were the Object of his Inquietude, and that he resented your Assiduities, which, I confess, have been too apparent to many.
>
> I Acknowledge myself to be jealous; and the Explanation I received from you yesterday, is so far from easing me of my Suspicions, that it has only contributed to increase them.
>
> No, my Lord, my Resolution is fix'd, and I am determined to see you no more.
>
> How irresistable is the Power of Love! I am convinced of your Guilt, and yet find myself compelled to pardon you!
>
> As much Love as you please, but a little more Discretion, or I am undone.[4]

She records, analyzes, and wallows in her feelings; like a true epistolary character, she does not simply recall things felt at other times, but in the writing itself, simultaneously describes and creates what she experiences.

These are typical contents for a form which took characters' thoughts and emotions (and the process of writing them out) as the plot-line rather than their acts. It was more important for a writer in this genre to depict realistically the movements of a mind than to dream up fabulous creatures and exciting plot twists. As Mrs. Manley explains in the preface to one of her books, the "Genius" of such an author was in discovering subtle emotional shifts and "those almost imperceivable Jealousies which escape the Sight of most Authors, because they have not an exact Notion of the Turnings and Motions of Humane Understanding; and they know nothing but the gross Passions, from whence they make but general Descriptions."[5]

Readers must have wanted to read minute descriptions of dissatisfactions, reconciliations, whims, resentments, for advertisements always emphasized the passion, the sentiment, to be found between the covers of a novel. The reading public no longer seemed to want the outlandish adventures of romances. Nor did they demand the trappings of verisimilitude in these stories flooded by the anguish of their characters. They simply wanted to read about how persons of quality felt about the sexual and economic conflicts in their lives and how they handled them.

But writing about emotional realities is a peculiar process because it changes those realities. So fictions based on the sentiments which characters write to one another become complicated, willy-nilly, by the ways in which that writing affects experience, lights it up. Awareness of events or emotions is intensified by re-experiencing them through the imagination. As Kierkegaard's poet-lover in *Repetition* found, living through experience a second time in the writing of it, raised "his own consciousness . . . to the second power."[6] Proust, with his sublime understanding of the power of imagined experience, describes the effect of repeating events on consciousness with this metaphor: "Pleasure," he says, "is like photography. What we take, in the presence of the beloved object, is merely a negative film; we develop it later, when we are at home and have once again found at our disposal that inner darkroom, the entrance to which is barred to us so long as we are with other people."[7] According to Proust, lived experience is but the raw material for that which is properly finished in memory—a process recorded in epistolary fiction.

Certainly within these novels, characters use their letters to re-live moments they have spent together. Not concerned with narrative progress, they describe to each other the episodes they have lived through together, dwelling on them in loving, repetitious, detail. In a novel by Eliza Haywood, for example, Theano recalls in a letter to his mistress Elismonda the night he "obtained the last favor" from her:

> Even in the most extatick Moment of Delights, when all dissolved, and melting in my Arms, you yielded Joys which Sense could hardly bear, I had but half been blest, had not the Truth, the Zeal, the Delicacy of my Love, made me conscious I was not altogether unworthy of the Bounty, and that it would be lasting as it was great.[8]

But Elismonda was there, too, living through those moments with him. When she describes her perceptions of the event in her return letter, it becomes clear that these separated lovers are substituting consciousness for sex and are having their relationship in words:

> How unsuspicious of your Design I suffer'd you to entertain me there, 'till falling Darkness dispers'd the Company, and the still Solitude of the silent Night encourag'd you to make an Attempt, by Day my Blushes might have oblig'd you to desist! . . . quite powerless, and depriv'd by these destructive Passions, of all Means of Defence, I suffer'd every Encrouchment your rapacious Love could make, 'till it had all obtain'd and I was wholly lost![9]

It is clear enough that letter writing in epistolary novels quickens infatuation quite as much as the passion inspires the writing. Epistolary lovers are always seducing themselves into melting thoughts of love by writing about their feelings. Nor are they unaware of these inflammatory effects. The Marchioness de M*** writes: "Ah me! into

what Extreams would my Emotions betray me, had I no
Subject for my Letter but this!" But once she writes of love
she is bewitched. "Why have I not the Power to erase these
Confessions . . ." she wonders.[10] We see her writing her
way deeper and deeper into desire before our very eyes. In
Love-Letters Between A Nobleman and His Sister, Sylvia
also gets carried away as she writes to Philander, and all
her good resolutions evaporate: "'Twas not my Purpose,
not my Business here, to give a Character of *Philander,* no
nor to speak of Love; but oh! like *Cowley's* Lute, my Soul
will sound to nothing but to Love: Talk what you will,
begin what Discourse you please, I end it all in
Love. . . ."[11] Olinda, too, another epistolary heroine, realizes that her dreamy ruminations on love, which allowed
her thoughts free rein—"the strongest Part of myself"—
was most dangerous of all:

> Had I had you my Friend to assist me with your Counsels, I had
> found it much less difficult; but now I had the *strongest Part of
> myself* to combat without any Aid: I often gave Ground, and
> sometimes suffer'd myself to be vanquish'd by the bewitching
> Reflections of what unequal'd Satisfaction I had found in his
> Company, and how many happy Hours I enjoyed with him.[12]

These are inevitable effects in a genre where, for the
most part, thought *is* action, and characters *are* their words.
"Be my letters the Test of your Passion," writes an epistolary lover. "If they are acceptable I must be so. . . ."[13] A
person is a reflection of his letters: they are a representa-
tion of him and can stand for him. People in epistolary
novels are always falling in love with each other, sight
unseen, on the strength of their letters. In *Olinda's Adventures: or, The Amours of a Young Lady,* for instance, an
early specimen of the form by Catherine Trotter, the
heroine writes such a moving love letter (though she only
writes it to practice her technique) that it causes one man to
fall in love with the passionate sensibility her writing

displays, and in another episode furnishes proof for her enemies of her abandoned immodesty.

In one epistolary novel a man even becomes obsessed with the heroine of another: a character in *Memoires On The Court of England* reads the ardent letters of Marianne, the Portuguese Nun, and mistaking what appears in the pages of a book for the real thing, falls madly in love with the intense creature. His friends try to rescue him from this hopeless infatuation by pushing him into another match, but he insists that this new woman they have found for him must write something for he cannot commit himself to love unless his literary sensibility is first moved. His friends think it odd "that a *Billetdouce* only of the *Portugueze* Lady's writing should make you fall in love,"[14] and suggest that he go "to *London*, where you may see, in Person, the Lady for whom you suffer so much already, perhaps there you will find better Employment, than to enquire after her writing well or ill."[15] But since he is not so interested in what she is like in person as he is in her prose style, the lady's writing is solicited. It comes to the literary-minded gentleman with this amusing note:

> You are never to be satisfied, and if the young Portugueze writ day and night, I question whether you would be contented and let me be at rest. You would do well to put some bounds to your Desires, because she is a little inclin'd to Laziness; and I can't at this time send you anything of hers, except a small Novel....[16]

Poor man! he would have done better to fall in love with a more prolific writer, for his appetite for this woman's writings evidently outstripped her ability to produce them.

Here are the earmarks of epistolary fiction in exaggerated form: the extraordinary appeal of passionate prose, the focusing of a great, romantic, love on a distant and symbolic object, the assumptions that a woman's words reveal her true qualities and that self-involved scribblers are more sensitive, more amorous, more exciting, than characters who do not commit their feelings to paper.

But the story is not yet done. The small novel which the lady sends—in much the same way that ladies of earlier times might have sent their portraits in miniature to prospective suitors—is an interpolated tale of much interest. It is about an escapade in the lives of two close friends, known as Pamfilia and the princess, who entertain themselves by disguising Pamfilia as a man and encouraging a certan Camilla to fall in love with her. The brief courtship is executed in writing, so the conspirators have a good time reading and writing the letters. However, when Pamfilia uncovers the earlier, real and tragic love affair of the misled Camilla, the novel abruptly ends. That is, as soon as Pamfilia decides to drop her verbal disguise, to stop fostering the love intrigue in writing from the safety of her assumed identity, the story is over and the small novel commissioned by the long-distance lover reaches its conclusion. Clever Pamfilia is an image of the author and when she stops transforming her world with her imagination, the novel, which is the ultimate example of such transformation, stops.

Camilla's own story—the tale within the tale within the tale—is also one of love, disguise, and letters. Camilla's suitor (a man of high degree, of course) disguises himself as a dancing master in order to gain Camilla's presence. When her father discovers the fraud, he plans to kill the man. Camilla then warns her lover in an impassioned letter, pleading with him to leave the country. He acquiesces in a short, broken-hearted answer.

It is Camilla's letter to the forbidden suitor which most impresses the man who commissioned the novel in the first place. The author, Donna Maria, writes it as if it were from Camilla's pen, but the eager reader takes it as proof of Donna Maria's sensitivity, her balance of passion and delicacy, and even of some secret and unhappy lover in her own past. When the novel first arrives and is read, the man's friends, still scoffing at his desire for a mistress who writes passionately, tease him by asking:

> What, don't you praise this little Novel? Don't you relish it? Or, do you want still another piece of *Donna Maria*, to support your resolution of loving her?[17]

The suitor-buyer-reader answers that he is satisfied with what he has read, and adds, excitedly,

> But don't you see, as well as I—that the whole is her own History, and that she has only represented it under borrow'd Names and fix'd the Scene in another Country.[18]

We have come full circle. The pretended fiction writer writes of real life, out of her own experience. That part of her fiction which gives her away, in particular, are the letters of passion, which strike the reader as being too life-like not to be authentic. And it is with this smolder-ingly passionate woman that the character in this story falls in love—with the woman who can write like that because she can feel like that. The writer is the heroine; the heroine is the writer. It is a perfect epistolary arrangement. We admire a character for the way in which she collects and presents her experience of herself. Yet this character exists only as a self-portrait about whom the reader must make his own inferences.

At all levels in this story, it is assumed that truth will out in writing (especially the direct, autobiographical writing of letters). The man who commissioned the story in the outer frame could only love a woman who would let him see her writing, for he was convinced that a truer self would be revealed to him in distilled form on paper than he could fathom in a face-to-face interview. Similarly, it was the keen edge of truth in Camilla's letter to her endangered lover which collapsed Pamfilia's fiction and cut through the rest of Donna Maria's novel to reach the heart and prove the point of the man who believed a woman's essence could be discerned in her words. The fiction is pervaded with the certainty that one cannot dissemble on paper, that once trapped into the act of writing, there is nowhere to hide—no way to simply smile and be impersonal and neutral. Words always express something of the self, give something away, share something with the reader.

Certainly the reader was meant to believe that the characters in such epistolary fictions were transcribing uncensored streams of consciousness. Thoughts are seemingly written down as they come, without any effort to control their logic or structure. Characters talk to themselves, reflect, think out loud—on paper. As a late eighteenth-century epistolary character wrote, "a letter is the soul's portrait. It is not like a cold image, with its stagnation, so remote from love; it lends itself to all our emotions; turn by turn it grows animated, it enjoys, it rests. . . ."[19] Héloïse herself said much the same thing about her prized letters from her beloved Abelard:[20]

> If a Picture, which is but a mute Representation of an Object, can give such Pleasure what cannot Letters inspire? They have souls, they can speak, they have in them all that Force which expresses the Transports of the Heart; they have all the Fire of our Passions, they can raise them as much as if the Persons themselves were present; . . . Letters were first invented for comforting such solitary Wretches as my self. Having lost the substantial Pleasures of seeing and possessing you, I shall in some measure compensate this loss, by the Satisfaction I shall find in your writing. There I shall read your most secret Thoughts; I shall carry them always about me, I shall Kiss them every moment. . . write always to me carelessly, and without Study: I had rather read the Dictates of the Heart than of the Brain.[21]

This equivalence between a person and his or her words sheds some light on those epistolary plots which center on persuasion. For in this genre, wherein a character *is* the written evidence of consciousness, any attempt to change that consciousness is a serious violation of identity. This kind of struggle is clear enough in stories of religious conversion or moral reform, but when any epistolary story is read carefully, it becomes apparent that some kind of subjective tug-of-war is going on. Whether the embattled characters in these stories are being pressured by parents, priests, politicians, or importunate lovers, they are generally caught in circumstances which are mentally and spiritually trying rather than physically dangerous. Whatever the object, the action is invading, exposing, uncovering things whose very existence depends upon their privacy; there are secrets to be kept, maneuvers to be managed, favors to be won. This state of siege as it affects the minds of the heroes and heroines is often what intensifies their self-involved examinations of consciousness, creating the tension in an otherwise inactive plot.

Certainly seduction, a standard plot in the epistolary novel, can be seen as an attempt of one person to change another's mind, an attempt to enter the consciousness, tamper with it, and reverse the intentions of the will. Particularly in epistolary novels, in which so much of the action happens in letters rather than in the bedroom, an actual sexual encounter is less to the point than the psychological capitulation which precedes it. Seduction then becomes a matter of will power rather than desire—a measure of who dominates whom rather than an occasion for physically forced compliance. Although there is an occasional Clarissa-like case of drugging, most of the violent attempts are on a woman's consciousness, not her body. It does not matter, therefore, that so many women in these stories are locked up in nunneries where they can only be reached by letters, since gentlemen in epistolary novels attempt to seduce from long distance rather than rape at close range. As Freud points out, the essence of virginity is mental anyway, a "demand that the girl shall bring with her into a marriage with one man no memory of sexual relations with another"[22]—the extension of ownership to a past and to a mind.

Similarly, the struggle of a character to preserve his or

her own private consciousness is frequently what is at the root of the religious dilemmas one finds so frequently in English epistolary fiction.[23] Catholic nuns and novices are regularly depicted as being unwilling to submerge their essentially Protestant imaginations in a more universal fantasy of Christian satisfaction.[24] They chafe against the public and communal life of the nunneries, thinking their own secret thoughts of love. They try to hang onto the private self which is essential to their daydreams of romantic love, setting themselves in opposition to an institution which is established to rob them of their individuality: to lock them up, to dress them alike, to purge each individual consciousness and fill it with communal thoughts.

Whether consciousness stands symbolically for sex or sex stands for consciousness, the fact is that the connection between consciousness and sexuality is very close in this genre where people are embodied in their correspondence. The contents of letters supposedly come from a deep wellspring of selfhood, and just as sexual union is seen as the sweeping away of constraints between individuals so that they are open and legible to one another, so the sharing of letters embodies great intimacy and trust. The power-conscious Mme. de Merteuil in Laclos' *Les Liaisons dangereuses*, for instance, never wrote to any of her lovers. She avoided creating any evidence of her indiscretions, and more importantly, never fully gave herself to anyone; she withheld that crucial thing, her writing, which would have given anyone power over her. In fact, her major error in the course of the book was disregarding that rule when writing honest letters to Valmont. If she had not loved him, if she had not written to him, she would have remained invincible.

Because letters reveal the self, reading the letters written and intended for other eyes is the most reprehensible invasion of privacy and consciousness in epistolary fiction. These are overtones of sexual invasion—of mind-rape—in the intercepting or "violating" of another's words. This equivalence is suggestive for the audience as well since they are reading letters not intended for public consumption. The most unholy thing in these books is uninvited access to another's inner life, and that is just what such novels offer, even in their very titles: *A Lady's Packet of Letters Broke Open; The Post-Boy Rob'd of His Mail; The Cabinet Opened.*

If the most regularly used symbol for the penetration of an individual's consciousness is sexual violation, and if it is the adamant protection of that individuality which stands symbolically at the heart of most of the sexual refusals in epistolary fiction, it is this that gives the reader a still clearer view of why these novels are structured as they are. Most early epistolary novels duplicate a woman's consciousness by providing her letters, and then allowing the audience to get inside it by reading those letters. The fact that the climax of the plot generally also had to do with "getting inside" a woman suggests that the sexual act works as a metaphor for the more important literary innovation—the getting inside of a woman's consciousness by the writer and by the reader.

There is a wonderfully vivid illustration of the implicit equivalence between a woman's writings and her person in the well-known scene in which Mr. B. tries to undress Pamela, ostensibly in order to get at the personal correspondence which Pamela has sewn into her clothes. Possessing her sexually is identified with possessing her thoughts, her words. The two goals are not distinguishable from each other and both signify dominion over her. That Pamela has to hide her letters on her body also dramatizes the fact that she has no territory to call her own except her own person. Her body and her consciousness are all that she possesses in the world and Mr. B. wants them both. The way they are combined in the plot is made evident by the way Mr. B. marries Pamela shortly after he takes possession of her letters and, therefore, her consciousness.

It is a tribute to Richardson's maturing and increasingly

original vision of human relations that the equation which
is so childishly obvious in *Pamela* is much more complicated in *Clarissa*. Clarissa's separation between her mind
and her body frustrates Lovelace's most profound attempt
to win her, and she is seen as preserving the inviolability of
her innermost thoughts (read soul), even though her body
has been raped.

Almost all epistolary novels make the assumption that
when a woman allows a man into her consciousness and
writes personal letters to him, sooner or later she will also
open her body to him. When a pursued heroine writes to
her pursuer, the reader knows immediately the outcome of
the chase. Valmont, the libertine in *Les Liaisons dangereuses*, understood this symbolic nature of letters, because
he always tried to inveigle his intended conquests into
writing to him at the beginning of his seductions. That
helped to insure his success—it was a symbolic foot in the
door. Writing a letter to a man was always the first step in a
girl's downfall, a preliminary to greater intimacies. One
epistolary character states this quite boldly: "I have at last
conquer'd the Maidenhead of your writing, as I hope one
day I shall that of your person."[25]

Perhaps letter writing was seen as an inevitable prelude
to sexual relations because writing permitted private intercourse between unmarried men and women in an era
which never allowed such unsupervised communication in
polite society. As a prude in Mary Davys' *Familiar Letters
Betwixt A Gentleman and a Lady* understood the social
rule, "writing to any Man, except a Husband, a Father, a
Brother, or some very near Relation, was an unpardonable
Crime, and cou'd not be answer'd to Modesty."[26] It was a
rule which arose in a culture with little unconstrained
interaction between the sexes, where the decorums of
unspokenness between men and women only served to
magnify the intimacies which people proffered to one
another when they wrote about themselves, making letter-
writing dangerous to chastity, an "unpardonable Crime."

"Good girls" in early epistolary novels—the ones who

exhibit only the most unsexual of emotions—rarely write directly even to the men they care most about. Melliora in *Love in Excess* does not write to her beloved D'Elmont at all, thus demonstrating her virtue.[27] Contrasted to this restraint is the freedom of the shameless hussy, the courtesan Ciamara, who writes to him several times enticing him in exactly the same spirit as she lures him into her bedroom and takes off her clothes. Sensitive ladies in such novels are even affronted by unsolicited letters written *to* them by suitors who do not bother to obtain permission to write. They treat the writing as if it were some kind of physical pawing. By the time of Fanny Burney's *Evelina*, just one unsolicited and familiar letter from even a favorite suitor was enough to damn the man in the eyes of the pristine heroine.

In life as well as in fiction, this anxiety surrounded the correspondence of a proper young gentlewoman. The following excerpt comes from a handbook on correct behavior for women and is part of an example of a model letter written by a young lady describing her life under the regimen of the perfect governess. The description states that the vigilant duenna

> aims not only at the benefit of our Bodies, but the eternal welfare of our Souls, in the Performance of our duties to God and our Parents. She continues her former jealousie [i.e. watchfulness], not suffering a Letter to come into the house without her Knowledge thereof; and herein her prudence is highly to be commended, for by her strict examination of these Paper-messengers, she shuts the doors against a great many which might be the Bawds that might betray the Obedience of some, and the Chastity of others. Neither are there any Answers returned to any Letters but what she is privy to; by which means, there is nothing we write we need be ashamed of, were it legibly written on our Foreheads as well as Papers.[28]

Because letters were so central to the conventional scenario of seduction, they had to be kept public, harmless, and scrutinized thoroughly by the guardians of a girl's honor.

The governess was expected to try to control everything that passed through a girl's mind.

Parents and other guardians of youthful virtue in epistolary novels always knew that the cabinet, the letter-writing desk, was the stronghold of consciousness and sexuality. It was from there that their charges created themselves and developed their intrigues. These young writers protected the privacy of that little space with as much assiduity as they protected their chastity for both had to do with selfhood. In fact, later in the century, Choderlos de Laclos makes the writing desk a painfully obvious symbol of chastity in *Les Liaisons dangereuses*. At the beginning of the book the young virgin, Cecile, keeps her *escritoire* well locked away from prying eyes. But when her privacy is rescinded—her key taken away and her *escritoire* no longer private—she herself is soon after seduced.

Indeed whenever protective parents in one of these novels wanted to find out what was going on with their children, they checked the innermost sanctuary: the child's writing cabinet. That is where true answers to parental questions were to be found. When the heroine of *The Agreeable Caledonian* would not marry the man her father had chosen for her, her clever and predictable parents went straight to her writing desk to see what was really happening in their daughter's life.[29] In *The British Recluse*, a friend of Cleomira's mother suggests that proof of Cleomira's fall from the strictest chastity might be had in her room. "I am afraid that your Daughter is in Love" she says. "I warrant if we shou'd search her Chamber we should find a number of amorous Books and epistles of the same Nature."[30] In *The Polite Correspondence* Eliza's father wants to know if she had been having an affair with a young man. He knows that by breaking into her desk he can find out what truths of her heart are most secretly hidden away. When he finds what he is looking for—a love letter—he promptly locks her up in her room. He is wrong, of course, to think that isolation will end the affair. For it is in isolation that Eliza gives her love and the forbidden letters which are the token of her person, to her young man. It is through these letters that we hear her story—these letters, which are the symbols and the expression of her individuality.[31]

In epistolary fiction, then, writing letters is a way of at least sharing oneself with another, and perhaps even creating a version of the self for that occasion. Thus it dramatizes the primary purpose of the novel, which is to make available to the reader another's state of consciousness. Most epistolary stories even raise the value of this kind of revelation by dramatizing the risks involved in such a discovery. Whether the immediate plot is one of parental pressure, spying, political intrigue, or sexual seduction, these tales often present another, more basic plot, one in which the self which has been created and revealed in letters protects and defends itself against all attempts at possession by others. Meanwhile, the reader, who has all along been reading the letters which tell the story, cannot help but be implicated in the exposure, the mind-rape, which is being acted out at the center of the book. We, parallel the villain's efforts to manipulate or possess the consciousness of the embattled heroes or heroines because we make our own efforts to get inside of them, to savor their essences, to see how they tick. This must partially account for the extraordinary interest of these fictions with their ritual characters and formulaic plots.

6

Romantic Love and Sexual Fantasy in Epistolary Fiction

It is not simple coincidence that the novel, and especially the epistolary novel, came into vogue at roughly the same time as women's preoccupations began to have less to do with how they actually lived their lives and more to do with the fantasies of love and romance which were the most they could expect as women, if they kept themselves graceful and attractive. The novel must be understood as a form of literature which developed at a time of dislocating social changes. The growth of cities and the beginnings of industrialism caused new divisions of function in the society on the basis of sex as well as class, and this seriously affected the condition of women in the literate classes. These city women no longer were the economic partners of men, for the new capitalistic modes no longer made public use of their labor, but separated them from the active concerns of life into a pretend world of romantic love and fantasy relationships. It is at this point that the novel came into its own—at a time in history when urban women of the middle and upper classes no longer had any economic power, when they no longer participated in the means of production of the society.

Novels fit into this changing social scene as the means for circulating the comforting affirmation that women were not meant to be grocers or haberdashers or wooldrapers (let alone doctors or scholars), but were intended solely for the business of romantic love. Indeed, if a novel had a male protagonist it could be about almost any sort of subject and circumstance, but if it was about a woman, it was almost certainly about her relation to a man; nothing else was germane. Most of these novels about women start as Thomas Brown's *The Adventures of Lindamira* (1702) does: "I shall pass over those little Occurances of my life till I arrived to my 16th Year, during which time nothing remarkable hapned [sic] to me," beginning at the point when the heroine becomes a sexually vulnerable figure, open to the temptations, delusions, and ecstasies of romantic love.[1]

The epistolary novel was the perfect vehicle for stories of romantic love because its very format demanded a subject matter in which emotional states were most prominent. Long distance epistolary involvements, like romantic love, required a taste for sentimentalized fantasy relations, and an ability to shut out humdrum reality. Created to seem possible and true to life, stories in letters portrayed characters who resembled their respectable readers, but who escaped their urban isolation by reading and writing their way into exciting amorous adventures.

Fantasies about love and marriage flourished in this environment not only because they justified the empty lives of middle and upper class women, but because the culture inhibited any realistic and easy relations between the sexes. Marriageable women were rarely alone with the men they imagined themselves to love; such a lack of access could only have encouraged idealized dreams of romance. Many courtships were carried on in letters fuelled by the imaginative process of writing, because written correspondence was the most direct and private way that unmarried men and women had of communicating with one another. We know, for instance, that John Evelyn's eldest daughter Elizabeth appalled her parents by eloping after a longstanding, clandestine correspondence. Dorothy Osborne and William Temple wrote to each other for seven years, despite his father's efforts to find a richer match as well as her relatives' disapproving judgment of William as an adventurer. Finally, after her father died and she survived the smallpox, which disfigured her, they married.

The danger of such relationships was that the distance made it easier to imitate the conventions of the fictions which furnished the ideal versions of such love affairs, and to ignore the obvious disparities between novelistic romances and the experiences of life. *The Spectator* warned, "We generally make Love in a Stile, and with Sentiments very unfit for ordinary Life: They are half Theatrical, half Romantick. By this Means we raise our Imaginations to what is not to be expected in humane life . . . because we did not beforehand think of the Creature we were enamoured of as subject to Dishumor, Age, Sickness, Impatience, or Sullennes. . . ."[2] As long as such romantic expectations had been attached only to those special relationships outside of the daily round of married life, the stories which promulgated them could have no pernicious effects. But in the fictions of love being written by the end of the seventeenth century, realistic characters were always working through crises, falling in and out of love, managing to live their lives at the emotional pitch which the new clichés about love and marriage celebrated, but which never quite came true for their readers.

The epistolary courtship of Dorothy Osborne and William Temple does not seem to have misled them, for their marriage appears to have been a contented one, despite their early prolonged separation. But other stories from real life did not end so happily. Lady Mary Wortley

Montagu, for example, enjoyed her courtship with Wortley and arranged to elope with him by letter, because she was forbidden to see him. Her clandestine correspondence, which ended in an unhappy marriage, is very dramatic, even reading like a novel. In fact, when she was an older woman she told her daughter that Richardson's *Clarissa* reminded her of her own youth. She wrote: "I was such an old Fool as to weep over Clarissa Harlowe like any milkmaid of sixteen over the Ballad of the Ladie's Fall [a broadside written circa 1680]. To say truth, the first volume soften'd me by a near ressemblance of my Maiden Days. . . ."3

And it is true—the letters from these "Maiden Days" do read like *Clarissa*. Lady Mary's parents tried to push her into a loveless marriage to add to the family's wealth, and although she argued and appealed to relatives to intercede for her, she finally had no other recourse but to make a stealthy escape. It was almost forty years before *Clarissa* when Lady Mary ran off with her lover; at that time most people did not yet consider love either a necessary or a sufficient condition for marrying. Lady Mary, who did not want to marry against her own inclinations, was advised to do so by her relatives, ordered to do so by her father, and considered "a little Romantic" by her friends. She was sure that even her friend Phillipa would think her mad to run away from an arranged marriage.

I give here most of the sequence which Lady Mary remembered so vividly in her later years, both for the sake of showing the degree to which fiction made use of the conditions of women's lives and because such an actual document throws some light on the fiction it resembles.

To Wortley, June 11, 1712:

> . . . My Family is resolv'd to dispose of me where I hate. I have made all the Opposition in my power; perhaps I have carry'd that opposition too far. However it is, things were carry'd to that height, I have been assur'd of never haveing a shilling, except I comply. Since the Time of Mandana's we have heard of no Lady's ran away with, without fortunes.4

To Wortley, July 26, 1712: she tells him that she has
written an importunate letter to her father and

> . . . said every thing in this Letter I thought proper to move him,
> and proffer'd in attonement for not marrying whom he would,
> never to marry at all. He did not think fit to answer this letter, but
> sent for me to him. He told me he was very much surpriz'd that I
> did not depend on his Judgement for my future happynesse, that
> he knew nothing I had to complain of etc., that he did not doubt I
> had some other fancy in my head which encourag'd me to this
> disobedience, but he assur'd me if I refus'd a settlement he has
> provided for me, he gave me his word, whatever proposalls were
> made him, he would never so much as enter into a Treaty with any
> other; that if I founded any hopes upon his death, I should find my
> selfe mistaken. . . . I told my Intention to all my nearest Relations;
> I was surpriz'd at their blameing it to the greatest degree. I was
> told they were sorry I would ruin my selfe, but if I was so
> unreasonable they could not blame my F[ather] whatever he
> inflicted on me. I objected I did not love him. They made answer
> they found no Necessity of Loveing; if I liv'd well with him, that
> was all was requir'd of me, and that if I consider'd this Town I
> should find very few women in love with their Husbands and yet a
> manny happy. It was in vain to dispute with such prudent people;
> they look'd upon me as a little Romantic, and I found it impossible
> to persuade them that liveing in London at Liberty was not the
> height of happynesse. . . .[5]

To Phillipa Mundy, August 1712:

> For my part, I know not what I shall do; perhaps at last I shall do
> something to surprize everybody. Where ever I am, and what ever
> becomes of me, I am ever yours. Limbo is better than Hell. My
> Adventures are very odd; I may go into Limbo if I please, but tis
> accompanny'd with such circumstances, my courage will hardly
> come up to it, yet perhaps it may. In short I know not what will
> become of me. You'l think me mad, but I know nothing certain but
> that I shall not dye an Old Maid, that's positive. . . .[6]

To Wortley, August 17, 1712:

> Every thing I apprehended is come t[o p]asse. 'Tis with the utmost
> difficulty [and d]anger I write this. My father is in the house. . . .
> I am frighted to death and know not what I say. I had the

precaution of desiring Mrs.— to send her servant to wait here for a
Letter, yet I am in apprehension of this being stopp'd. If tis, I have
yet more to suffer, for I have been forc'd to promise to write no
more to you.[7]

To Wortley, August 18, 1712:

. . .If you can come to the same place any time before that, I may
slip out, because they have no suspicion of the morning before a
Journey. Tis possible some of the servants will be about the house
and see me go off, but when I am once with you, tis no matter.—If
this is impracticable, Adieu, I fear for ever.[8]

To Wortley, August 18, 1712:

I would not give my selfe the pain of thinking you have suffer'd as
much by this misfortune as I have done. The pain of my mind has
very much affected my body. I have been sick ever since, yet tho'
overcome by fateigue and misfortune I write to you from the first
Inn. . . .[9]

The similarity of Lady Mary Wortley Montagu's experience to those of Richardson's celebrated heroine is star-
tling. It makes the interchange between art and life more
tangible: Richardson's art seems more geniunely borrowed
from the life of his day, while Lady Mary's letters seem
more dramatic than life usually is. The energy in these
letters comes not only from her fine independent spirit
dealing with difficulties, but also from the theatrical
touches in her writing which betray interest in the melo-
drama of her situation. The way she compares her plight
to that of Mandane in the romance by Scudéry, the
ironic self-consciousness of writing "Hell" to mean spin-
sterhood and "Limbo" for an uncertain elopement, and
the flamboyance of her declarations give one the impression that she thinks her life comparable to that of a fictional heroine.

The excitement of Lady Mary's courtship with Edward
Wortley Montagu must have been heightened by their
separation, by their constant brooding about one another,

and, of course, by the correspondence that they had to resort to. Their meetings had all the trappings of forbidden adulterous affairs: fear of suspicion, arrangements for passing letters, and for properly spaced meetings in larger gatherings. Their letters are all about missing each other, sudden jealousies, and the designing of future *tête-à-têtes.* Behind their relationship was the titillation of checking over one's shoulder, of defying parents, of living out a romance—all the elements of an epistolary relationship. The passion with which they invested their relationship was manufactured out of their fantasies about love and about each other rather than growing gradually out of direct experience of the other.

Lady Mary's marriage was evidently not a happy one, and she must have speculated on the degree to which the imaginings of love reckoned in her own youthful folly. Throughout her later letters she reiterates the maxim that passion keeps better in the imagination than in reality, that long possession of any woman inevitably cools a man's desire for her. In the wisdom of age, having lived through her own difficulties, her final response to Richardson's novel was unsympathetic. She wrote to her daughter:

> Even that model of Perfection, Clarissa, is so faulty in her behavior as to deserve little Compassion. Any Girl that runs away with a young Fellow without intending to marry him should be carry'd to the Bridewell or Bedlam the next day. Yet the circumstances are so laid as to inspire tenderness, not withstanding the low style and absurd incidents, and I look upon this and Pamela to be two Books that will do more general mischief than the Works of Lord Rochester.[10]

The mischief of which she spoke, no doubt, was the sort that followed from too close identification with such fictional heroines. Novels like *Clarissa* sowed false expectations of romance in young women, as well as such sympathy for her yearnings as might lead them to share her downfall. While Lord Rochester only wrote lascivious verses whose original impulse was clear and whose effects predictable, Richardson wrote books which lured the reader into a world in which right was not so very distinguishable from wrong, because the verisimilitude of the characterizations roused an empathy in the reader which confused the issues. The epistolary format, especially, created a genre in which each character spoke for him or herself, from his or her own point of view; as Clarissa put it to her friend Anna Howe: "there would hardly be a guilty person in the world, were each *suspected* or *accused* person to tell his or her own story and be allowed any degree of credit."[11]

The trouble was that there was not sufficient ballast in women's lives to keep their feet on the ground. The work they did became progressively more ornamental and less functional in the course of the seventeenth century. Like the heroines of epistolary novels, they merely filled their time while waiting for something exciting to happen. Elizabeth Pepys, for example, the wife of the famous diarist, suffered from having nothing to do while her husband was off with friends or at his office. Samuel Pepys seems to have understood what a strain such interminable inactivity was on his wife, although he could not do much about it:

> Up and began our discontent again, and sorely angered my wife, who indeed do live very lonely, but I do perceive that it is want of work . . . . Then to my office late, and this afternoon my wife in her discontent sent me a letter, which I am in a quandry what to do, whether to read it or not, but I propose not, but to burn it before her face, that I may put a stop to more of this nature. But I must think of some way, either to find her some body to keep her company, or to set her to work and by employment to take up her thoughts and time.[12]

With four or five servants and no children, Elizabeth Pepys had little to do but write complaining letters to her husband, who for his part was always hiring some new maid to keep his wife company, or taking her to visit her mother, or engaging a music teacher or a dancing master to keep her occupied.

The situation was no better for brave Lady Mary Wortley Montagu who wrote this letter to her new husband, describing her occupations in his absence:

> I write and read till I can't see, and then I walk; sleep succeeds; thus my whole time is divided. If I was as well qualified in all other ways as I am by idleness, I would publish a daily paper called the *Meditator*. . . . Till today I have had no occasion of opening my mouth to speak, since I wished you a good journey. I see nothing, but I think of every thing, and indulge my imagination, which is chiefly employed on you.[13]

Nor was her case unusual. The editor of *The Tatler* claimed he knew twenty families by name "where all the Girls hear of in this Life is, That it is Time to rise and to come to Dinner; as if they were so insignificant as to be wholly provided for when they are fed and cloathed." With an understanding rare to his time, he continued: "It is with great Indignation that I see such Crowds of the Female World lost to humane Society and condemned to a Laziness, which makes Life pass away with less Relish than in the hardest Labour."[14]

Woman's domain had been reduced to her own small nuclear family, for which she was provided with necessities (cloth, food) by professionals in a wage economy which increasingly excluded her. The new cultural emphasis on childhood and childrearing which Philippe Ariès dates from the end of the seventeenth century probably grew out of this social dysfunction. It was then that childhood began to be understood as qualitatively different from adulthood: children stopped beng dressed exactly like adults, and painters stopped paintng them as scaled-down adults.[15] The new consideration given to the education and training of children made motherhood into a kind of profession, creating new responsibilities for women, and providing them with new leverage within the evolving family.

But these were not roles which required formal education and rarely were women trained to read further than the semi-literate assortment of novels, romances, and plays available to them. Even wealthy women were expected to improve their time with needlework rather than in the pursuit of learning. Mary Astell, who petitioned Queen Anne to set up schools for women, felt that this cultural neglect of women's minds was the root symptom of the prejudice against them, and that to it could be traced their characteristic boredom, frivolity, and expense. An intellectual life was the highest good, she believed, and leisure was best filled with serious study and charitable works. She felt that women needed education to help right the balance in their lives, to promote reason over passion, and reality over fantasy. But in advocating women's schools, she could not always keep an ironic note from her writing, for she knew she was demanding it in a social vacuum:

> But to what Study shall we apply ourselves? some Men say that Heraldry is a pretty Study for a Woman, for this reason, I suppose, That she may know how to Blazon her Lord and Master's great Atchievements! They allow us Poetry, Plays, and Romances, to Divert us and themselves; and when they would express a particular Esteem for a Woman's Sense, they recommend History; tho' with Submission, History can only serve us for Amusement and a Subject of Discourse. [For] . . . how will this help our Conduct or excite us in a generous Emulation? since the Men being the Historians, they seldom condescend to record the great and good Actions of Women; and when they take notice of them, 'tis with this wise Remark, That such Women *acted above their Sex*. By which one must suppose they would have their Readers understand, That they were not Women who did those Great Actions, but that they were Men in Petticoats![16]

With so little to give their lives meaning and stability, it is no wonder that women were given to illusory brooding about romance. A sophisticated character in a French epistolary novel later in the century shuddered for the susceptibility of idle women whose energies centered on love:

> Tremble above all for those women, active in their idleness, whom you call "tender," of whom love takes possession so easily and

with such power; women who feel the need to occupy themselves with it even when they do not enjoy it and who, abandoning themselves unreservedly to the ebullition of their ideas, give birth through them to those sweet letters which are so dangerous to write; women who are not afraid to confide these proofs of their weakness to the person who causes them; imprudent women, who cannot see their future enemy in their present lover.[17]

"Those sweet letters" to which epistolary heroines abandoned themselves, were "dangerous to write" because they fanned the flames of love and encouraged solitary dreaming. Writing kept a woman on the string, imaginatively involved in the love affair, no matter what the distance, no matter what the obstacles. As the famous letter-writing Portuguese Nun observed: "a man should rather fix upon a Mistress in a Convent than anywhere else. For they have nothing there to hinder them from being perpetually Intent upon their Passion. . . ."[18]

The unreality of women's lives was also perpetuated by such training and direction as they did get. Lord Halifax's famous letter to his daughter, a distillation of the soundest precepts of his time, advised her "to have a perpetual watch upon your Eyes, and to remember, that one careless Glance giveth more advantage than a hundred words not enough considered."[19] He warned her to avoid gambling because she might get caught up in the game and forget to compose her face. Everywhere he reminds her that her reputation is her most important possession, in a hostile world where everyone is after her virtue. "The Enemy is abroad and you are sure to be taken if you are found stragling."[20] He preached constant vigilance and mastery of inference, of indirect expression, of innuendo. Indeed, his advice could also have been aimed at training for seduction, so much did he emphasize the possible effects of the smallest sign or gesture of real feeling.

Steele satirizes this trained coquetry in the complaints of a fashionable London lady about her visiting country cousin, in *The Spectator*.

> She is very pretty, but you can't imagine how Unformed a Creature it is. She comes to my Hands just as Nature left her, half finished, and without any acquired Improvements. . . . She knows no Way to express her self but by Tongue, and that always to signifie her Meaning. Her Eyes serve her yet only to see with, and she is utterly a Foreigner to the Language of Looks and Glances. In this I fancy you could help her better than any Body. I have bestowed two Months in teaching her to Sigh when she is not concerned, and to Smile when she is not pleased: and am ashamed to own she makes little or no Improvement . . . . I could pardon too her Blushing, if she knew how to carry her self in it and if it did not manifestly injure her Complexion.[21]

Although Steele humorously overdoes his thesis that city women are caricatures of all that is unnatural, always playing a part, still he suggests how genteel women of his time did violence to their own feelings of reality. He also describes the upbringing which trained them to control their feelings, expressions, and actions, to ignore discomfort for beauty, and to choose an immediate pain in the expectation of a future pleasure:

> When a Girl is safely brought from her Nurse, before she is capable of forming one simple Notion of anything in Life . . . [she] is taught a fantastical Gravity of Behaviour and is forced to a particular Way of holding her Head, heaving her Breast, and moving with her whole Body; and all this under the Pain of never having a Husband; if she steps, looks, or moves awry. This gives the Young Lady wonderful Workings of Imagination, what is to pass between her and this Husband, that she is every Moment told of, and for whom she seems to be educated.[22]

This is an important point: women were being brought up to live imaginatively in the future; nothing else in their lives justified such training as they got.

By assuming that women were meant primarily for romantic attachment, society condemned them to it. Gone were the earlier straightforward contractual relations between the sexes, supplanted by the mystification of idealized relationships. The only appropriate ambition of a lady of quality was to bend all efforts to the art of pleasing. This constant recourse to the judgments of others was to take the place of living for them and fill the gaps of education and career. " 'Tis much more natural for women to please men than do any other thing," states a pamphlet published in 1696. "And this desire which is so innate to the Sex, makes them live without action."[23] Women were instructed to treat themselves as mirrors, to reflect others rather than to have any self. They were to live in their imaginings of others' thoughts rather than in their own reality. "True Love," began "Mrs. Steele" ominously in the third volume of *The Ladies Library*, "in all Accidents, looks upon the Person beloved, and observes his countenance, and how he approves or disapproves it, and accordingly looks sad or cheerful."[24] Since love was to be the basic inspiration of a married woman's life, she was to experience everything in terms of another's wishes, and filter her life through the construct of her husband's mind.

Not only did this society demand that women move carefully and watchfully through life, guided by their conscious minds and not their instincts, but it denied their physical reality, the enjoyment of their bodies. Their visible constraint was even remarked by a foreign visitor:

> Walking is likewise a great Diversion among the Ladies, and their Manner of doing it is one way of knowing their Character; desiring only to be seen, they walk together, for the most part, without speaking: They are always dress'd, and always stiff; they go forward constantly, and nothing can amuse or put them out of their way; I doubt they would not stoop to take up a Flower from under their Feet: I never saw any of them lie on the Grass, not shew the least Inclination to sing. . . .[25]

The ultimate physical repression, of course, was the culture's denial of female sexuality. Although trained to attract men, even in a sexual way, the love women were to bear their husbands was to exclude the natural reason that men and women mate. The author of *The Present State of*

Matrimony suggested that women have *"an inexpressible Desire of Children,* which we rudely, and wrongfully term Lust . . . This Passion for young Children, is beyond Imagination. The most chaste Virgin in the World can scarce contain herself at the Sight of a beautiful Child; but is ready to devour it with her Kisses."[26] Any feeling more distinctly physical than that in a woman was thought degenerate. Many critics have taken Clarissa's vacillations as a sign of her neurosis, but it was characteristic of the period to assume that women only endured sex for money or security. Even Moll Flanders only used sex for these ends. The early novels are filled with heroines who are woodenly unconscious of their own desire—a convention which demonstrated their decency and modesty as well as the expectations of polite society. Defoe, who chides his male readers in *Conjugal Lewdness* for marrying solely for "Money and Maidenhood," never admits the possibility of women's marrying for sexual reasons. But he does warn prospective husbands that they would be fools to marry any woman who granted the ultimate favor before the wedding night, because such appetite proved them unfit for marriage.

These attitudes had not always prevailed—even in England. In Chaucer's time, for example, the sexuality of that gat-toothed woman, the libidinous Wife of Bath, was portrayed without embarrassment, ugliness, or shame. Her lustiness was a sign of vitality and readers were to delight in it, to admire her for having had the world in her time. In the Renaissance, too, a woman's sexual appetite was recognized and even feared. For once she was introduced to sexual pleasure by her conjugal duties and her natural passion aroused, one could not depend on her chastity. Husbands were therefore advised to limit sexual activity with their wives, "even to the point of deprecating pleasure,"[27] and not awaken this dangerous appetite. Certainly the Renaissance conventions of adulterous passion, a system which separated love from marriage, implicitly

recognized women's desires. But by the eighteenth century, decent women were no longer expected to enjoy their
sexuality. In 1714 a woman, shielded by anonymity,
lamented in *The Spectator* " that Men may boast and glory
in those things that we must think of with Shame and
Horror!"[28]

The public promotion of contraceptives made this denial
all the more double-edged inasmuch as it clarified the
distinction between sex for pleasure and sex for reproduc-
tion. Although contraceptives had been used in many
cultures for centuries, public notice of them was new.[29]
The first mention of them in print came in 1708, in *The
Charitable Surgeon*, by "T. C. Surgeon" (pirated from
John Marten) which offered "The certain easy way to
escape Infection, tho' never so often accompanying with
the most polluted Companion," and went on to hint that it
might keep young ladies from "a great belly."[30] A year later
The Tatler jogged the public memory by touting him who
"invented an Engine for the Prevention of Harms by Love
Adventures" as a great "Promoter of Gallantry and Pleasure."[31] These notices amounted to a public recognition
that sex could be indulged in exclusively for pleasure.
Indeed, Defoe frowned upon their use in marriage as
encouraging improper attitudes towards sexual relations.[32]

It is important to know these facts about women's lives if
one is to make sense of Clarissa's endless ambivalence,
Pamela's investment in her simple style of dress, the
interminable letters which they wrote, or the reading
public's fascination with long stories of women's seduction. The speakers in many early novels were women: Moll
Flanders, Roxana, Pamela, Clarissa, Evelina; and their
moral, economic, and social choices were symbolized
almost exclusively in sexual terms because increasingly,
that *was* the only option in women's lives. Unlike the
dazzling but faceless damsels of earlier romances, these
self-involved heroines focused minutely and lengthily on
their own feelings, for they evolved when their genteel

counterparts in life were bored, inactive, badly educated, and without real work. It is no wonder that women's lives furnished the materials for a genre whose subject matter was deferred experience and emotional description. But the inventors of such heroines had to be careful not to outrage polite readers of their fictions. Their characters had to have the fire and imagination for the ardent love affairs readers wanted to experience by proxy, but enough discretion to inhibit these impulses like properly bred women. The solution was to let art imitate life, and to portray women who enacted in fantasy what they were denied in actuality. One of Mrs. Manley's heroines, for instance, confides to her lover that

> Fancy has brought you near, nay so very near, as to my Bosom; there this Morning I dream'd you were, and the Imagination was so strong, that starting out of my Sleep I left my Dream imperfect; my Senses, had their Concern been less, had not so soon rous'd themselves to find whether the Object were a real or imaginary Happiness. And I perhaps had longer seen you, nay, I more than saw you, forgive the Pleasure I take in writing freely....[33]

The unconsciousness of the dream state not only relieved her of responsibility for her sexual desire, but also proved her moral strength. For virtue is cheap if there is no passion to overcome, no struggle to win. Héloise's letters, too, report living through moments from the past she shared with Abelard in a precious, recurring dream:

> During the still Night, when my Heart ought to be quiet in the midst of sleep, which suspends the greatest Disturbances, I cannot avoid those Illusions my Heart entertains. I think I am still with my dear Abelard. I see him, I speak to him, and hear him answer. Charmed with each other, we quit our Philosophick studies to entertain ourselves with our Passion....[34]

The dream itself is about surrender to passion, the relaxation of vigilant reason, that moment when a woman puts down her book and stops studying. And that is when the remembrance comes to Héloise—when her guard is down, when her fantasies are available to her, unlocked by sleep. As Eliza Haywood told her readers "whatever Dominion, Honour, and Virtue may have over our waking Thoughts, 'tis certain that they fly from the clos'd Eyes, our Passions then exert their forceful Power, and that which is most Predominant in the Soul, Agitates the fancy, and brings even Things Impossible to pass: Desire, with watchful Diligence repell'd, returns with greater violence in unguarded sleep, and overthrows the vain Efforts of Day."[35] Haywood herself has a delightful example of it in *Love in Excess*, when during her sleep "Melliora in spite of herself, was often happy in Idea, and possest a Blessing, which shame and Guilt deter'd her from in reality."[36] We see Melliora enact in dumbshow, still asleep, the motions of her desire while calling out: "too too lovely Count— Ecstatic Ruiner!" What is all the more delicious, the Count himself is present in the room with her, holding her and kissing her as she sleeps. Melliora can enact her impulsive desires but without any moral responsibility for them because she is asleep. Meanwhile, the chaste reader, too, could have the satisfaction of both admiring an honorable heroine and of vicariously enjoying her less-than-honorable embraces.

Such a scene testifies to the increasing gap in early eighteenth-century culture between private sexual indulgence and public emphasis on chastity; it shows the hypocrisy of an age in which men had the reputations of libertines, while women denied and were denied their sexuality. Nor was the effect of this public prudery to dismiss questions of sex from the public consciousness but rather to focus it more sharply on the mildest of actions. By the time Fanny Burney wrote *Evelina*, her readership was titillated by the effrontery of a man who took the arm of a decent woman unbidden. Innuendo and metaphor began to make up the deficits in explicit storytelling in these stories of thwarted love: when Melliora stuffs the keyhole to her room to prevent the Count from using his key, there is no doubt about what these images stand for; the nun in Jane Barker's *A Patch-work Screen For The Ladies* touches off a fire in her convent as she runs away with her lover—the convent and her passion simultaneously burst into flames.

Inevitably, it was feared that such reading would have bad effects on the suggestible minds of young women who were learning to read in greater numbers all the time. Take this warning, for example, the donné of a story by Jane Barker: wealthy Dorinda is so blinded and misled by the romantic fiction with which she has been filling her head that she makes the terrible mistake of marrying her footman, sure that he is a prince in disguise. However once he has the legal prerogatives of a husband he proves to be a brute, taking over her property and even pushing her out of the house. She finally blames fiction for the illusions which led her into folly.

> It was such Romantick Whimsies that brought upon me the Ruin and Distress in which you behold me; I had read Plays, Novels and Romances; till I began to think myself a Heroine of the first rate; and all Men that flatter'd, or ogled me were Heroes; and that a pretty well-behaved foot-man or Page must needs be the Son of some Lord or great Gentleman.[37]

In Defoe's *The Family Instructor* (1715), the exemplary dialogue between mother and daughter focuses on this problem as if it were a standard reason for the maternal admonitions of young ladies. At the end of the ideal scenario between mother and daughter, the repentant daughter makes an enormous bonfire of all her plays, romances, and novels, in a blaze of religious fervor. The transgressions of the son in this fictively typical family were profligacy, drinking, play-going, and swearing; no one was concerned about the delicate balance of *his* mind. Not until fifty years later was there a male character, Rousseau's St. Preux, who was encouraged in his deceptions about romantic love by reading too many novels.

Parents recognized that novels set improper examples and encouraged improper feelings, that the passions in these fictions "are apt to insinuate themselves into unwary Readers, and by an unhappy Inversion a copy shall produce an Original. . . . Indeed 'tis very difficult to imagine what vast Mischief is done to the World by the False Notions and Images of Things, particularly of Love and Honour, those noblest concerns of Human Life, represented in these Mirrors."[38] In fact, epistolary fictions were always calling the attention of readers to these dangers. It was as if they advertised their product and testified for it themselves. In a conversation in *Love in Excess*, it was averred that "these sort of Books were, as it were, preparations to Love, and by their softening Influence melted the Soul, and made it fit for Amorous Impressions."[39] In other words, one was more open to real sexual experience if one had lived through it once already in the imagination.

There is a letter in the fictional collection, *The Post-Boy Rob'd of His Mail*, in which a libertine instructs a complicitous maid by letter to help him time his amorous attacks:

> Watch her softest hours, when her Soul's in tune to join with the Harmony of Love: After her Mind has been employed in Romances, Plays, and Novels, then nought but sweet Ideas fill her Soul, and Love can't be denied admittance, those having so well prepared the way.[40]

He subscribes to the theory that these stories of love will stimulate the woman's sexual impulses and he wants to strike, so to speak, when the iron is hot. In another fiction, an experienced woman writes a letter to a friend, in which she describes seducing a young man by lending him some books. The volume that seemed most effective, significantly enough, is a collection of letters:

> We chanced one day to light upon Brown's Translation of *Fontenel's* and *Aristaenetus's* Letters; he seem'd mightily pleas'd

> with 'em; there was one from a Lady who permits a Lover all but
> the Last Favor, and gives him leave to touch her Breast, to Kiss her
> Eyes, her Mouth, and squeeze her with her stays off; he could not
> imagine what Pleasure could be taken in that. . . .[41]

Certainly the epistolary author is asking the reader-at-
home to "imagine what Pleasure could be taken in that," as
well as telling the story. Books do lead one into sexual
thoughts. The sequence is reminiscent of Dante's lovers
Paolo and Francesca seduced by the kiss in their book.
Needless to say, the heroine soon shows the naif what he
has been missing. But it is clear that the seeds of his
seduction were planted not by any real touching, but by the
imagined touching which he experienced through the
printed page. This is the point at which the experience of
the reader in the fiction is shared exactly by the reader-at-
home.

The same seductive technique is employed by the Duke
in the *Secret Memoirs . . . from New Atalantis* when, attracted to his beautiful young ward Charlot, he decides to
stop playing guardian to her virtue and to corrupt her. Like
Milton's Satan, he knows that the surest way is to appeal to
her imagination, to offer the intangible. He leads her to the
library and directs her to read romances and novels and
various works which focus on love. Then he leaves for
several days, to give the poison a chance to work:

> The Duke was an Age absent from her, she could only in
> Imagination possess what she believed so pleasing. Her Memory
> was prodigious, she was indefatigable in Reading. The Duke had
> left Orders she shou'd not be controul'd in any thing: Whole
> Nights were wasted by her in the Gallery; she had too well
> inform'd her self of the speculative Joys of Loves. There are Books
> dangerous to the Community of Mankind; abominable for Virgins,
> and destructive to Youth; such as explains the Mysteries of Nature,
> the congregated Pleasures of Venus, the full Delights of mutual
> Lovers, which rather ought to pass the Fire than the Press.[42]

The episodes which follow are predictable. Charlot
succumbs to temptation and becomes the Duke's mistress

upon his return. Advertising her book as the apotheosis of passion, Mrs. Manley unconsciously burlesques the scene, promising her readers a "young and innocent Charlot, transported with the powerful Emotion of a just kindling Flame, sinking with Delight and Shame upon the Bosom of her Lover in the Gallery of Books."[43] It is a wonderful image, a perfect emblem of the warning and fascination for books which describe love, illustrating how stories about passion induce passion, that vicarious experience enjoyed in the reading could have consequences in real life.

Again and again in epistolary novels, there are scenes which do not advance the plot but seem especially prepared, garnished, and served as inducements to fantasy. Reported in letters, they are twice as suggestive, for they carry with them the motives of the fictive correspondents who want to re-experience their moments of passion by writing about them. Sylvia, for instance, in *Love-Letters Between A Nobleman and His Sister,* writes to her lover:

> What tho' I lay extended on my Bed undrest, unapprehensive of my Fate, my Bosom loose and easy of Access, my Garments ready, thin and wantonly put on, as if they would with little Force submit to the fond straying Hand. . . .[44]

There is no narrative reason for Sylvia to tell Philander all this since both he and his "fond straying Hand" were present at the time. The reader can only understand it as a daydream, a delicious moment Sylvia wants Philander to live through again with her in the imagination. But the passage is also designed to allow the audience a chance to imagine themselves into such a moment. Another letter-writing character, almost as blatant, urges his sister to think of him at the moment he takes his new bride to bed: "I conjure you, Sister, by our Friendship, in your Imagination to time my Joys, when all transported I shall naked clasp her fair, soft, sweet, enchanting Body to my Bosom. . . ."[45] Such letters are explicit invitations to the reader-at-home, too, to indulge in voyeuristic fantasy.

Imagine, for instance, a solitary reader at home in 1730 reading these words written by a solitary character having an epistolary love affair:

> The thoughts of your Return, and our happy Meeting again, fills me with Ideas too ravishing to admit Allay. . . . Instead of amusing myself with any thing that might make me forget you, I take no Delight but in remembering you: Recollections presenting me with ten thousand nameless Softnesses your dear Society blest me with, and I injoy them over again in Theory. . . .[46]

The unspecific language could fit almost anyone's fantasy of love. And the reader could certainly "injoy them over again in theory" as often and as imaginatively as the epistolary heroine herself.

Even the plot structures of epistolary novels have a sexual rhythm, building towards the moment of sexual release. "I could grow old with waiting here the blessed Moment," writes Philander in *Love-letters Between a Nobleman and His Sister*, focusing his entire attention, and the reader's as well, on that moment.[47] The characters in epistolary novels stimulate and tease themselves, as well as the reader, with their longings for one another, their jealousies, and the possibilities of their next meeting. The culmination of this epistolary activity is usually their sexual union, the non-verbal end to which the writing is directed. The hindrances to this consummation, the obstacles in the way, then become a kind of titillating foreplay the author and reader engage in. As one of Mrs. Manley's epistolary characters asks, "what can be more exquisite than delay'd Enjoyment?"[48]

In Aphra Behn's *Love-Letters Between A Nobleman and His Sister*, for instance, although we know from the start that Philander and Sylvia are destined for each other, three quarters of Part I goes by before they manage to go to bed together. Until then, most of their writing has to do with the planning and anticipation of that moment. Many pages, written to tantalize and heighten the suspense, elapse after

Sylvia agrees to it. And then, after all that, Sylvia faints and Philander becomes impotent; the tryst is a failure and the lovers begin to plan for another one. And so the novel itself becomes a paradigm of sexual play: building up the audience for the big moment, delaying it, and building up again.

The same rhythm is worked out in Eliza Haywood's *Love in Excess*. Many times before the dénouement, the sexual act is averted at the last minute. The would-be lovers are interrupted at the crucial moment many times and finally even separated by nunnery walls before the actual reunion and marriage take place. There is even one scene in which the Count, about to be seduced by a wealthy, corrupt, alluring woman, is saved at the eleventh hour when a messenger bursts into the room. The scene is unintentionally laughable, for the Count has already come to the brink of intercourse so many times with the lovely Melliora that his near seduction seems like an unintended parody of those scenes: virtue is always being saved just in the nick of time. Not that there is ever any question about the eventual outcome. One of the characters even carries around a wedding gown in a trunk, as Haywood carried the ending in her mind from the start, and makes a dramatic entrance in it at the triple marriage which ends the book.

Interestingly, overt pornography was developing at the same time as these epistolary tales of love and sex. Certainly they came out of the same socio-economic facts: growing literacy and book production, an increased emphasis on women as sexual objects along with greater restraints than ever on their availability, and arrangements for privacy in urban dwellings. This was a context which bred a taste for sexual fantasy, and in it the pornographic novel grew up side by side with the polite novel.

There had always been a place for the bawdy in literature, for the telling of dirty stories for raucous enjoyment. But this new kind of book had a very different effect on its readers. Here is an account which Pepys gives of finding a copy of *L'Ecole des Filles* unexpectedly:

Jan. 13, 1668

. . . stopped at Martin's, my bookseller, where I saw the French book which I did think to have had for my wife to translate, called 'L'escholle des filles,' but when I come to look at it, it is the most bawdy, lewd book that I ever saw, rather worse than 'Putana errante,' so that I was ashamed of reading it.[49]

But the fascination outlasted the shame, and a month later Pepys returned to his bookseller's shop and

. . . bought the idle rogueish book 'L'escholle des filles,' which I have bought in plain binding, avoiding the buying of it better bound, because I resolve, as soon as I have read it, to burn it, that it may not stand in the list of books nor among them, to disgrace them if it should be found.[50]

The next day, having read his new book, Pepys says that

it is a mightly lewd book, but yet not amiss for a sober man once to read over to inform himself of the vilany of the world. . . . I to my chamber where read through 'L'escholle des filles,' a lewd book, but what do no wrong once to read for information sake. . . . And after I had done it I burned it, that it might not be among my books to my shame, and so at night to supper and to bed.[51]

Pepys's response to the book distinguished it from the bawdy of earlier periods: by 1668 sexuality had the power to entice and to shame. It counted among the villainies of the world, and a reader had to somehow justify his reading such books by claiming for them some redeeming social value.

Both pornography and novels shared an emphasis on the flammable imagination, on the dimension of mental activity in sexual matters. But whereas polite prose fiction emphasized women's sexuality by means of prudish abhorrence of it, by imagining women as protectors of the honor of their families, pornographic books were exclusively about the other side of women's nature. *La Puttana Errante* (1650) was a discussion between whores on the means to sexual pleasure; *L'Ecole des Filles*, published five years later, linked sex to romantic love in a radical departure from conventional mores. By 1660 there was a book out which specialized in perversions, including sections on the young, group intercourse, whipping and lesbianism.[52] Women were viewed as angels in one form of prose fiction and as whores in another—in both cases in exclusively sexual terms.

Epistolary fiction, in which characters tried expressly to share their experiences with one another, capitalized on these trends. After all, the purpose of a letter is to make one person's consciousness available to another. Epistolary characters are always trying to make people far away catch fire, to make their friends and lovers feel what they feel. Sometimes this intention is explicit, as with Edward Ward's young man who employs "*Loves* common confidant, The *Pen*" as a "means of kindling the like Desires in my new found Angel. . . "[53] Or there is Mary Davys' gentleman who also thinks a pen the most effective way to woo a lady. "Methinks," replies this man's intended victim, warning him that she is not susceptible to his sweet words, "you write as if you had a mind to draw me in, as you pretend Love has done you, by Wheedle."[54]

Since all the relationships in an epistolary novel are verbal, people fall in love with one another's words, tempt each other at long distance by writing seductive things, and spy on each other's words. The novels set out to dramatize the relation of imagination to life, the way the words on a page can play havoc with the emotional state of a reader. And because the novel reader is also privy to these very powerful words, he or she is also open to their effects.

Indeed, epistolary fiction often encouraged readers' identification by providing a third figure in the novel who also read the letters, who was privy to the action, and who comprehended the intimacy between the major correspondents. This third person, sometimes a confidante of the hero or heroine, sometimes part of a love triangle, opened up the tale to the reader-at-home by doubling his or her role as spectator to the emotional action.

There is an example of this provocation to voyeurism in *The Unnatural Mother and Ungrateful Wife,* a story in which daughters triumph over their mothers. It comes in a central scene in which the kindly woman who is being betrayed by her adopted daughter is alerted to this state of affairs by her waiting maid. She watches through a keyhole and sees her husband come into evil Nelly's room at midnight "with nothing on him but his Shirt and a Night-Gown flowing loose about him." Then the faithless man "threw himself on her Bosom with eager Haste, seem'd ready to stifle her with burning Kisses, while his wanton Hands were preparing to consummate the last guilty Rites of lawless Passion."[55] As the betrayed wife watches the two lovers enact their passion, the reader notices, with a kind of jealous and guilty shock, that he or she is also watching. The scene, then, is structured to duplicate, for the reader, the voyeurism and to intensify the feelings it engenders.

René Girard, writing theoretically about the novel, describes and explains this "triangulation of desire" as he calls it.[56] Triangulating desire, arranging a three-way love interest rather than a simple two-way mutual attraction, keeps the desire from being a simple, direct relation between the one who loves and the object of desire. A triple relationship is mediated by someone else's responses, and this mediation, this awareness of a third person's implication in the love affair intensifies the desire, for the rivals imitate each other, reinforce their own fixations by imagining the other's feeling. In other words, the force of triangular desire comes from the mind, as it were, rather than from the viscera; its power can be attributed to the intensified consciousness which jealousy provokes. Such triangulation is almost standard in epistolary novels, in which letters between lovers or confidantes are always being forged, intercepted, or even just read, legitimately, by a third person.

The experience of vicariously sharing the lives of fictional characters is undoubtedly familiar to long-time novel readers. By now we have all grown up knowing that feeling of becoming absorbed in another world, of escaping through the printed page, of going into that reading trance which substitutes the reality of the world on the page for the world around us; but this is a relatively recent notion of the way literature can function. It was not until the early epistolary novels, with their long-distance relationships, their emotional realism, their stories of amateur writers trying to let one another in on essential experiences, that books were turned to such a use. Until then literature was used to delight and to instruct, but not to confound a storybook realm with real life.

Nor were books the proper medium for light entertainment until literacy and book production put them in the hands of a much larger proportion of the population. Printed literature had always been the province of a small number of educated aristocrats until the late seventeenth century, with traditions going back to the Bible or the classical writers. The issues of these novels—the search for personal happiness in romantic love and marriage, and the sanctification of the individual consciousness (the resistance to seduction or persuasion, the need for privacy)—these had not mattered to earlier cultures. Not until the economic and cultural changes of the seventeenth century, with the consequent reshaping of community and family life, altered social patterns was there need for a literature with another audience, another purpose, another set of strategies.

One of the earliest critics to consider the "origin and progress of novel-writing," the first editor of Richardson's letters, describes what is special about the way Clarissa works:

> We do not come upon unexpected adventures and wonderful recognitions, by quick turns and surprise: we see her fate from afar, as it were through a long avenue, the gradual approach to

which, without ever losing sight of the object, has more of simplicity and grandeur than the most cunning labyrinth. . . As the work advances, the character rises; the distress is deepened; our hearts are torn with pity and indignation; bursts of grief succeed one another, till at length the mind is composed and harmonized with emotions of milder sorrow; we are calmed into resignation, elevated with pious hope, and dismissed glowing with the conscious triumph of virtue.[57]

Moment by moment the experienced novelist guides us into a world which is familiar and simplified. Gradually he draws us into believing in it, meshes its assumptions with our own, arranges for us to live in his world long enough until it takes over our entire consciousness and "our hearts are torn with pity and indignation" and all the rest of it.

In letter fiction, because writer and reader are already part of the fictional reality, a reader-at-home is that much closer to full suspension of disbelief. Whereas in the epics or tragedies of the Greeks, *catharsis* was achieved by ritual progress through symbolic action, here it is achieved by identification with the particular plight of a particular individual. We feel the dilemma because we care for Clarissa. The participatory *action* of reading letters, the attempt to re-create the world of the letter-writer so as to make sense of the letter, encourages this empathy. And for the reading audience of these early novels, used to maintaining emotional connections with family and friends by mail for long periods of time, the effort must have been a familiar one.

Letters have the natural property of suspending attention from the world of objects and turning it inward to imagined people and relationships. These attention-riveting qualities of letters are apparent simply by picking up a modern day letter manual and skimming some samples. The words on the page, with their implication of direct, personal communication, have the power to take precedence over the immediate world. It is not necessary to have a personal connection to the circumstances of these writings to participate in the fictional world from which they arise; one naturally tries to fill in the qualities of the letter-writer and the relationship with the interlocutor from the tone and style of the letter.

These effects influenced the developing novel. A fiction presented "unedited" in a series of letters could lure a reader into putting the story together, into caring about the characters behind the letters. The adventures and relationships of solitary letter-writing characters in fiction were more available to solitary readers at home for delectation and escape than those offered in a more conventional narrative form. Letter novels, like letters themselves, could take you vicariously where you could not go in life.

But this could also be a moral advantage, as Richardson convinced the reading public. One could live through others' mistakes and emerge unscathed but chastened. The experience of an exemplary consciousness—that of a Pamela or a Clarissa—could inspire, uplift, change a reader. "Many a young woman has caught from such works as *Clarissa* or *Cecilia*, ideas of delicacy and refinement which were not, perhaps, to be gained in any society she could have access to," wrote Anna Letitia Barbauld in her early nineteenth-century eulogy of Richardson. In an ancedote included in the introduction to the second edition of *Pamela*, this sorcery of the novel, this power to take over the reader, is held up as its special advantage:

> The first Discovery we made of this Power over so unripe and unfix'd an Attention, was, one Evening, when I was reading her [Pamela's] Reflections at the *Pond* to some Company. The little rampant Intruder, being kept out by the Extent of the Circle, had crept under my Chair, and was sitting before me, on the Carpet, with his Head almost touching the Book, and his Face bowing down toward the Fire.—He had sat for some time in this Posture, with a Stillnes, that made us conclude him asleep: when, on a sudden, we heard a Succession of heart-heaving Sobs; which while he strove to conceal from our Notice, his little Sides swell'd, as if they wou'd burst, with the throbbing Restraint of his Sorrow. I turn'd his innocent Face, to look toward me; but his Eyes were quite lost, in his *Tears*. . . .[He] is perhaps the youngest of *Pamela's Converts.* [58]

This passage is a testimonial to the novel's success, proof that it has the desired effect, that it can do its appointed job properly. That stillness which seemed like sleep is a sign of the spellbinding, the transfixion of the boy in another consciousness. The fact that we are told he also "has got half her sayings by heart, talks no other language but hers..." demonstrates, too, the extent to which he has entered Pamela's mind, or perhaps let her enter his. A new era of fiction had begun; now a book was expected to do more than just tell a story.

Letters, by virtue of their place in the culture, their literary effects, and their implicit fiction of a single, personal voice, had been an important link in the process which evolved the modern novel. The experience of long-distance correspondence made it possible for the reading audience to imagine carrying on an emotional life at some remove, or to maintain a one-sided relationship in the imagination rather than to live it out in the social world. This new kind of literature encouraged readers to dream themselves into the lives they found in books, lives of characters for whom reading and writing were their most significant acts.

The epistolary mode also made plausible a new kind of heroine—literate, isolated, unhappy—who symbolized in a purer form the dilemmas of the current culture than the heroes of earlier romances and epics. Such heroines, who poured out their hearts on paper, valued their individual happiness above social approval and assumed that this happiness was to be found not in work or religion but in a perfect sexual union whose institutional form was marriage. These were assumptions which, however widely adopted by middle-class English society, belonged particularly to the women of that class, for the economic and social reorganization which took place in England in the course of the seventeenth century had abridged many of their functions. Novels not only filled the leisure of those without serious work but provided romantic fantasies to give meaning to their lives. Even the intoxication of reading novels resembled the intoxication of romantic love; the epistolary formula, in particular, was a perfect one for stories of romantic love ending in "happily ever after" marriages. In this way, epistolary novels perpetuated the myth of romance in everyday life by telling such stories as if they were true, by giving them wider circulation and making them part of the popular culture, and by inviting readers in their very form, to partake of the pleasures of fantasy.

Notes

CHAPTER 1
Letter Fiction and the Search for Human Nature

1. J. H. Plumb, *England in the Eighteenth Century* (Harmondsworth, 1950), p. 17.
2. W. Maitland, *A History of London* (London, 1739), pp. 322–324.
3. M. Dorothy George, *London Life in the Eighteenth Century* (New York, 1965), pp. 10–11.
4. Philip Pinkus, *Grub Street Stripped Bare* (New York, 1968), p. 285. This is quoted from a contemporary broadsheet.
5. Margaret Cole, *Marriage: Past and Present* (London, 1938), p. 86.
6. Ronald Paulson, *Hogarth: His Life, Art and Times*, 2 vols. (New Haven, 1971), I, 254.
7. David Owen, *English Philanthropy* (Cambridge, Mass., 1964), p. 53.
8. M. Dorothy George, *London Life in the Eighteenth Century*, p. 25. See the work of early demographers such as John Graunt and William Petty or the pamphlet *Marriage Promoted: In a Discourse of Its Ancient and Modern Practice both under Heathen and Christian Commonwealth* (London, 1690), described below.
9. William Black, *Observations Medical and Political on the Small Pox and the Mortality of Mankind at Every Age in City and Country* (London, 1781), p. 154.

10. Ernst Cassirer, *The Philosophy of the Enlightenment*, trans. Fritz C. Koelln and James Pettegrove (Princeton, 1951), p. 47.

11. Marjorie Nicolson and Nora Mohler, "The Scientific Background of Swift's Voyage to Laputa," *Annals of Science*, 1937, II, 299–334. See especially pp. 322–323.

12. César de Saussure, *Lettres et Voyages* (Laussane, 1903), Lettre VI, pp. 166–167.

13. Ronald Paulson, *Hogarth: His Life, Art, and Times*, I, p. 92.

14. William M. McBurney, *A Checklist of Prose Fiction, 1700–1739* (Cambridge, 1960), p. viii.

15. E. S. de Beer, ed., *The Diary of John Evelyn* (London, 1959), p. 689. Entry dated August 27, 1680.

16. *Ibid.*, p. 1027.

17. These newsletters were like the European *relations* or reports of topical events. See Joseph Frank, *The Beginnings of the English Newspaper, 1620–1660* (Cambridge, 1961).

18. For Ward's sensational "letters" describing the pleasure-seekers of Tunbridge or the wicked colonists of New England, see Edward Ward, "A Packet from Will's" in *Letters of Love, Gallantry, and Several Other Occasions*, 2 vols., by Voiture, Brown, Dryden, Congreve, etc. (London, 1724) II; also *A Trip to New England* (London, 1699). This and "A Letter From New England" are reprinted by the Club for Colonial Reprints, ed. George Parker Winship (Providence, 1905).

19. John J. Richetti, *Popular Fiction Before Richardson: Narrative Patterns 1700–1739* (Oxford, 1969), p. 77.

20. *Ibid.*, p. 77.

21. Philip Pinkus, *Grub Street Stripped Bare*, p. 92.

22. Eliza Haywood, *The Agreeable Caledonian* (London, 1728), p. 84.

23. Thomas Salmon, *A Critical Essay Concerning Marriage* (London, 1724), p. 165.

24. Eliza Haywood, "Good Out of Evil; or, The Double Deceit" appearing in Eliza Haywood, *Love in Its Variety; Being a Collection of Select Novels written in Spanish by Signior Michael Bandello* (London, 1727), p. 67.

25. Mary Delariviere Manley, *The Secret History of Queen Zarah* (London, 1705), Preface.

26. *Ibid.*, Preface.
27. A *Spy Upon the Conjurer,* author uncertain, possibly Daniel Defoe or Eliza Haywood (London, 1724), Part III.
28. Eliza Haywood, *The Disguis'd Prince or, The Beautiful Parisian* (London, 1728), pp. 1–2. This is a translation of a French book written in 1679 by Jean de Préchac.
29. Pierre Corlet de Chamblain de Marivaux, *The Life of Marianne* (London, 1736), Part II, 83–84.
30. Robert Adams Day, *Told in Letters* (Ann Arbor, 1966), p. 71.
31. A. S. Collins, 'The Growth of the Reading Public During the Eighteenth Century," *Review of English Studies,* II(1926), 284–294.
32. Mary Davys, "Familiar Letters Betwixt a Gentleman and a Lady," in *The Works of Mrs. Davys,* 2 vols. (London, 1725), II. Also available in publications of *Augustan Reprint Society,* #54, 1955.
33. William Henry Irving, *The Providence of Wit in The English Letter-Writers* (Durham, 1955), p. 145.
34. David Nichols, *The Correspondence of Dean Atterbury,* 5 vols. (London, 1783–1790), I, iv.
35. *The Spectator,* No. 632, Dublin, Nov. 30, 1714.
36. *The Complete Letters of Lady Mary Wortley Montagu,* ed. Robert Halsband, 3 vols. (Oxford, 1965), I, Appendix I, 467.
37. *Ibid.*, p. 467.
38. Robert Day, *Told in Letters,* pp. 239–258.
39. This is Day's figure. Actually there were somewhat fewer for some of the works on his bibliography are duplicates: the same book reprinted later with a new title page, or individual pieces of a collection listed individually and also together.
40. An unpublished Radcliffe thesis by Ruth Stauffer in 1942.
41. Mme. D'Aulnoy, *The Present Court of Spain,* trans. Thomas Brown (London, 1693), Preface.
42. *The Spectator,* No. 4, March 5, 1711.
43. *The Spectator,* No. 10, March 12, 1711.
44. *The Diary of Dudley Ryder (1715–1716)* ed. William Matthews (London, 1939), p. 119. Entry dated October 14, 1715.
45. George Frisbie Whicher, *The Life and Romances of Eliza Haywood* (New York, 1915), p. 11.
46. Robert Day, *Told in Letters,* p. 74.

47. *Marriage Promoted: In a Discourse of Its Ancient and Modern Practice both under Heathen and Christian Commonwealth*, anonymous pamphlet (London, 1690), p. 27.
48. *The Works of Mr. Thomas Brown*, 2 vols. (London, 1707), I, 337–340.
49. "Captain Ayloffe's Letters," in Abel Boyer's *Letters of Wit, Politics, and Morality* (London, 1701), reprinted in Natascha Würzbach, *The Novel in Letters* (Coral Gables, 1969), p. 27.
50. Aphra Behn, *Love-Letters Between A Nobleman and His Sister* (London, 1694), Part I reprinted in Natascha Würzbach, *The Novel in Letters*, p. 206.
51. *Ibid.*, p. 217.
52. *Five Love-letters From a Nun to a Cavalier*, trans. Sir Roger L'Estrange (London, 1678), reprinted in Natascha Würzbach, *The Novel in Letters*, p. 17.
53. Anonymous, *The Fatal Amour Between a Beautiful Lady and a Young Nobleman* (London, 1719), p. 64.
54. Chapter 2, *passim*.
55. Reprinted in Natascha Würzbach, *The Novel in Letters*, p. 221.
56. *Ibid.*, p. 215.
57. *Ibid.*, p. 265.
58. *Ibid.*, p. 225.

CHAPTER 2
The Economic Status of Women

1. For a encyclopedic discussion of the development of the modern nuclear family durng this period see Lawrence Stone, *The Family, Sex and Marriage* (New York, 1977), pp. 123–269.
2. Austin Lane Poole, *Obligations of Society in the Twelfth and Thirteenth Centuries* (Oxford, 1946), pp. 51, 43, 72, 74.
3. Sir Frederick Pollack and Frederick W. Maitland, *History of English Law* (Cambridge, 1918). Summarized by Mary R. Beard, *Woman as Force in History* (New York, 1946), pp. 186–192.

4. F. W. Tickner, *Women in English Economic History* (London, 1923), p. 53.

5. "A new Method for making Women as useful and as capable of maintaining themselves, as the Men are; and consequently preventing their becoming old Maids, or taking ill Courses", *Gentleman's Magazine*, 9 (1739), 525.

6. The *O.E.D.* also dates the word "henpeck" to the late seventeenth century.

7. *The Spectator*, No. 295, February 6, 1712. See also *The Tatler*, No. 199, July 18, 1710.

8. Thomas Salmon, *A Critical Essay Concerning Marriage* (London, 1724), p. 210.

9. A letter written home to France in 1726 describes the following advantage of this law for debtors. Evidently, a woman under peril of imprisonment for heavy debts could go to Fleet Street and find there a boy or man already detained for his debts, with no hope of getting out, and pay him three or four guineas to marry her on the spot. Then off went the woman, with her new marriage certificate, and when her debtors tried to collect from her, she proved that she was married and therefore that her husband assumed her debts. Meanwhile, her "husband" was already in jail for his hopeless debts, and the frustrated collectors could not get any money from him either. César de Saussure, *Lettres et Voyages* (Laussance, 1903), Lettre XV, pp. 365-366.

10. Thomas Salmon, *A Critical Essay Concerning Marriage*, p. 210.

11. John Newton, *Women's Position Before English Law, from Anglo-Saxon Times Until Today* (London, 1899).

12. *Ibid.*

13. Peter Laslett, *The World We Have Lost* (New York, 1965), p. 12.

14. F. W. Tickner, *Women in English Economic History*, (London, 1923), p. 132.

15. J. H. Plumb, *England in the Eighteenth Century* (Harmondsworth, 1950), p. 20.

16. Not only is this privacy/solitude essential to the paradigm of the letter writer, but it is related to changing courtship patterns as well. See Lewis Mumford, *The City in History*, (New York, 1961), pp. 382–385. Ian Watt also speaks of the

place of the inevitable individual isolation and privacy of city living in the origins of the novel. See Ian Watt, *The Rise of the Novel* (Berkeley, 1957), pp. 178–179, 185–187.

17. Christopher Hill, *Society and Puritanism in Pre-Revolutionary England* (London, 1964), p. 448.
18. *The Spectator*, No. 500, October 3, 1712. For a discussion of the patriarchal family in England, see Lawrence Stone, *The Family, Sex and Marriage*, pp. 123–150.
19. Peter Laslett, *The World We Have Lost*, p. 57.
20. Christopher Hill, *Society and Puritanism in Pre-Revolutionary England*, p. 448.
21. Thomas Salmon, *A Critical Essay Concerning Marriage*, p. 15.
22. Andrew Browning, ed., *English Historical Documents 1660–1714* (London, 1953), VIII, 325.
23. *Marriage Promoted: In a Discourse of its Ancient and Modern Practice both under Heathen and Christian Commonwealths* (London, 1690), pp. 11–12.
24. F. W. Tickner, *Women in English Economic History*, pp. 104, 115. See also Barbara Ehrenreich and Deirdre English, *Witches, Midwives, and Nurses, A History of Women Healers* (Old Westbury, N.Y., 1973), p. 18; Ivy Pinchbeck, *Women Workers in the Industrial Revolution* (London, 1930) pp. 44, 306, 315, 375, and *passim*; Eric Richards, "Women in the British Economy Since About 1700", *History*, 59(1974), 337–357.
25. Statutes of the Realm, v. II, 380. Quoted in Eileen Power, *Medieval Women* (Cambridge, 1975), p. 64.
26. Alice Clark, *Working Life of Women in the Seventeenth Century* (London, 1919), pp. 138–145.
27. J. H. Plumb, *England in the Eighteenth Century*, p. 22.
28. William Alexander, M. D., *A History of Women*, 2 vols. (London, 1782), II, 111.
29. *O.E.D.* under *spinster*.
30. For a discussion of the household arts deemed necessary even in noble women during the Renaissance, see Ruth Kelso, *Doctrine for the Lady of the Renaissance* (Urbana, Ill., 1965), pp. 111–115, 121.
31. F. W. Tickner, *Women in English Economic History*, pp. 67–68.

32. R. Reuss, *Londres et l'Angleterre en 1700*, quoted in M. Dorothy George, *London Life in the Eighteenth Century*, p. 169.

33. *Pehr Kalm's Account of His Visit to England* (1748), trans. Joseph Lucas (London, 1892). Letter dated April 11, 1748, pp. 327–328.

34. *The British Journal*, Saturday, November 3, 1722.

35. William Black, *Observations*, p. 238.

36. M. Dorothy George, *London Life in the Eighteenth Century*, p. 172. There is an appendix which lists the occupations and wages of married couples, pp. 427–429.

37. Mary Astell, *Some Reflections upon Marriage* (London, 1700), p. 174.

38. E. S. de Beer, ed., *The Diary of John Evelyn* (London, 1959), p. 831. Entry dated October 26–28, 1685.

39. *The Friendly Society for Widows: being a Proposal for Supplying the Defect of Joyntures and Securing Women from falling into Poverty and Distress at the Deaths of Their Husbands* (London, 1696).

40. *The Complete Letters of Lady Mary Wortley Montagu*, ed. Robert Halsband, 3 vols. (Oxford, 1965), I, 277. Letter from Lady Mary to Lady X on October 1, 1716.

41. George Wheler, *A Protestant Monastery* (London, 1698), pp. 14–15.

42. *Ibid.*, p. 15.

43. John Ashton, *Social Life in the Reign of Queen Anne* (London, 1897), pp. 18–20; Myra Reynolds, *The Learned Lady in England 1650–1760* (Boston, 1920), pp. 258–268; Josephine Kamm, *Hope Deferred* (London, 1965), pp. 68–101.

44. Mary Astell, *The Christian Religion as Profess'd by a Daughter of The Church of England* (London, 1705), p. 141.

45. *The Diary of Samuel Pepys*, ed. Henry B. Wheatley, 2 vols. (London, 1893), I, 560.

46. Jane Barker, *A Patch-work Screen For The Ladies* (London, 1723), p. 79.

47. "A Letter to a Young Lady on her Marriage" (1723), *Satires and Personal Writings by Jonathan Swift*, ed. William A. Eddy (London, 1933), pp. 59–72.

48. See, for example, his column in *The Tatler*, No. 32, June 18, 1709 where he collapses Mary Astell and Mrs. Manley into the figure of one ridiculous "learned lady."

49. *The Earlier Life and the Chief Earlier Works of Daniel Defoe*, ed. Henry Morley (London, 1889), p. 144.

50. Mary Astell, *A Serious Proposal to the Ladies* (London, 1694).

51. *The Complete Letters of Lady Mary Wortley Montagu*, ed. Robert Halsband, 3 vols., (Oxford, 1965), I, 270. Letter to Lady Rich, September 20, 1716.

52. William Sewel, *History of the Christian People Called Quakers* (London, 1722), quoted in I.B. O'Malley, *Women in Subjection* (London, 1933), p. 125.

53. William C. Braithwaite, *Second Period of Quakerism* (London, 1919), quoted in I.B. O'Malley, *Women in Subjection*, p. 128.

54. I.B. O'Malley, *Women in Subjection*, p. 128.

55. Mary Astell, *Some Reflections Upon Marriage* (London, 1700), p. 28.

56. Mary Davys, "Familiar Letters Betwixt a Gentleman and a Lady," in *The Works of Mrs. Davys*, 2 vols. (London, 1725), II, 303. Also available in publications of Augustan Reprint Society, #54, 1955.

57. Philogamous, *The Present State of Matrimony* (London, 1739), p. 53.

58. *The Spectator*, No. 573, July 28, 1714.

59. E. S. de Beer, ed., *The Diary of John Evelyn*, p. 272. Entry dated September 10, 1647.

60. Peter Laslett and others have recently made the case that the average age of marriage for women was in their early twenties, and for men, roughly five years later. He states that nobles to establish alliances between powerful houses maried younger than the pragmatic marriages of the lower classes, but reports that he found very few cases of thirteen, fourteen, fifteen year olds among the license records kept in various dioceses. One must remember, however, that until civil law regulated legal marriages in 1753, all such records were incomplete. Peter Laslett, *The World We Have Lost* (New York, 1965), p. 82. Also see *Population In History*, ed. D. V. Glass and D. E. C. Eversley (London, 1965), *passim*.

61. Ian Watt, *The Rise of The Novel*, p. 158.
62. Thomas Salmon, *A Critical Essay Concerning Marriage*, pp. 35–36.
63. Béat de Muralt, *Letters Describing the Character and Customs of the English and French Nations* (London, 1726), p. 66.
64. "The Lady's New Year's Gift, or Advice to a Daughter", *The Life and Letters of Sir George Saville, Bart. First Marquis of Halifax*, 2 vols., ed. H. C. Foxcroft (London, 1898), II, 388–424. This manual of behavior was first written in 1678, but went through many editions all the way through the eighteenth century. It is a first-rate source on attitudes towards women at that time, because it was written in earnest by a concerned and loving father, and because it was popular for so long.
65. Samuel Richardson, *Letters Written To and For Particular Friends on the Most Important Occasions* (London, 1741), Letter LV, p. 68.
66. *The Diary of John Evelyn*, ed. E.S. de Beer, p. 336. Entry dated May 11, 1654.
67. M. Phillips and W. S. Tomkinson, *English Women in Life and Letters* (Oxford, 1926), pp. 116–123.
68. Mary Astell, *The Christian Religion as Profess'd by a Daughter of the Church of England*, p. 113.
69. *The Spectator*, No. 4, March 5, 1711.
70. Philogamus, *The Present State of Matrimony* (London, 1739), p. 25.
71. Eliza Haywood, *Love in Excess* (London, 1719), pp. 5–6.
72. *Ibid.*
73. Mary Delariviere Manley, *Secret Memoirs and Manners of Several Persons of Quality of Both Sexes From New Atalantis* (London, 1709), p. 63.
74. Eliza Haywood, *The Fatal Secret* (London, 1724).
75. Pierre Corlet de Chamblain Marivaux, *The Life of Marianne* (London, 1736).
76. Anonymous, *The Unnatural Mother and Ungrateful Wife* (London, 1730).
77. H. J. Habakkuk, "Marriage Settlements in the 18th Century," *Transactions of the Royal Society*, 4th Series, XXXII(1950), pp. 15–30. See also Ian Watt, *The Rise of the Novel*, pp. 142–148.

78. *Marriage Promoted: In a Discourse of Its Ancient and Modern Practice both under Heathen and Christian Commonwealths*, (London, 1690), p. 52.
79. Karl Marx, *The German Ideology, 1845–1846*, trans. 1965 (New York, 1965), pp. 192–193.
80. John Campbell, *The Polite Correspondence*, 3 vols. (London, probably 1730), III, 202.
81. *The Letters of Abelard and Héloise*, trans. & ed. John Hughes (London, 1743), p. 101.
82. Mary Delariviere Manley, *Secret Memoirs and Manners of Several Persons of Quality of Both Sexes From New Atalantis*, p. 65.
83. See, for example, *The Spectator*, No. 268, January 7, 1712 or *The Spectator*, No. 511, October 16, 1712.
84. Daniel Defoe, *Conjugal Lewdness: or Matrimonial Whoredom* (London, 1727).
85. Peter Laslett, *The World We Have Lost*, 142 ff.; Lewis Stockton, *Marriage, Civil and Ecclesiastical*, (Buffalo, 1912), pp. 22–25.
86. F. W. Tickner, *Women in English Economic History*, p. 101; John Ashton, *Social Life in the Reign of Queen Anne*, pp. 22–23.
87. César de Saussure, *Lettres et Voyages* (Laussance, 1903), Lettre XV, pp. 365–366. See above p. 173, n. 9.
88. D. B. Horn and Mary Ransome, eds., *English Historical Documents, 1714–1783* (London, 1957), X, 242.
89. Anonymous, *Letter from a By-Stander* (London, 1753), p. 7.
90. *Ibid.*, p. 10.

CHAPTER 3

The Social Context of Letters

1. R. W. Chapman, "The Course of the Post in the Eighteenth Century," *Notes and Queries*, 183(1942), pp. 67–69.
2. William Maitland, *History and Survey of London* (London, 1739), Book V, 631.
3. Daniel Defoe, *A Tour Thro' The Whole Island of Great Britain*, 3 vols. (London, 1726), reprinted in a limited edition

with an introduction by G.D.H. Cole (London, 1927), I, Letter V, 343–344.

4. César de Saussure, *Lettres et Voyages* (Lausanne, 1903), Lettre VI, p. 158; *Pehr Kalm's Account of His Visit to England* (1748), trans. Joseph Lucas (London, 1892), p. 63; M. Mission, *Memoirs and Observations in His Travels Over England*, trans. Ozell (London, 1718), p. 222.

5. Robert Day, *Told In Letters* (Ann Arbor, 1966), p. 49.

6. *The Spectator*, No. 581, August 16, 1714.

7. Ernst Cassirer, *The Philosophy of the Enlightenment*, trans. Fritz C. Koelln and James Pettegrove (Princeton, 1951), p. 4.

8. *The Diary of Dudley Ryder*, ed. William Matthews (London, 1939), p. 29.

9. *English Historical Documents*, ed. Andrew Browning (London, 1953), VIII, 328.

10. *The Spectator*, No. 619, November 12, 1714.

11. Robert Day, *Told in Letters*, p. 79.

12. See, for example, Aphra Behn, *Love-Letters Between A Nobleman and His Sister* (London, 1694), or Eliza Haywood, "The Witty Reclaimer or A Man Made Honest" from *Love in Its Variety* (London, 1727).

13. "Dr. Drake's Character of Thomas Brown," prefixed to *The Works of Thomas Brown*, 2 vols. (London, 1707), I.

14. Thomas Brown, *Letters From the Dead to the Living* (London, 1702).

15. Benjamin Boyce, Brown's biographer, thinks a woman may have collaborated with Brown on this pleasant novel. He argues that there is no record of Brown's claiming the novel, that possibly his name was used to sell the book, and that "the story is presented, moreover, from the feminine angle: in it a clever woman's untaught ingenuity and inherent fineness lead her safely through many trials. . ." He does not think a man could have given such a "decent" or "delicate" picture of feminine conduct, such a "proper" story, or such a "refined analysis of feminine character." But he does think Brown collaborated on it and supplied the element of which a woman would be incapable: the humor. See Benjamin Boyce, *Tom Brown of Facetious Memory* (Cambridge, 1939), pp. 106–108.

16. Virginia Woolf, *The Second Common Reader* (New York, 1932), p. 51.

17. *Ibid.*, p. 52.

18. Béat de Muralt, *Letters Describing the Character and Customs of the French and English Nations* (London, 1726), p. 82.

19. *The Diary of Dudley Ryder*, April 23, 1716, p. 225.

20. The "celebrated Toast" was not merely a figure of speech, for in 1703 Lord Wharton wrote the following for the Kit Cat Club:
> Fill the Glass; let the Hautboys sound,
> Whilst bright Longy's Health goes round:
> With eternal Beauty blest,
> Ever blooming, still the best;
> Drink your Glass, and think the rest,

Swift's warm words were written on December 22, 1711, upon hearing of her death. Jonathan Swift, *Miscellaneous and Autobiographical Pieces, Fragments, and Marginalia*, ed. by Herbert Davis and Basil Blackwell (Oxford, 1962).

21. Robert Day, *Told in Letters*, p. 65.

22. *Letters Written by Mrs. Manley*, 2nd edition (London, 1713), Dedicatory Epistle.

23. William Henry Irving, *The Providence of Wit in the English Letter-Writers* (Durham, 1955), p. 145.

24. Preface to the quarto edition of Alexander Pope's *Letters* (1737), in *Correspondence*, ed. George Sherburn, 5 vols. (Oxford, 1956), I, xxxviii–xxxix.

25. Charles Gildon, *The Post-Boy Rob'd of His Mail* (London, 1692), p. 9.

26. *Letters Writ by a Turkish Spy*, 8 vols., trans. William Bradshaw and Robert Midgeley (1687–1694) from G. P. Marana's *L'espion Turc* (1685–1686) went through many editions and in 1718 Daniel Defoe came out with *A Continuation of Letters Writ by a Turkish Spy at Paris*. David Jones, *The Secret History of White-Hall* (London, 1697); L. S. Ratisbone, *An Account of the Secret Service of M. de Vernay* (Amsterdam, 1683); Eliza Haywood, *A Spy Upon the Conjurer* (London, 1724); Anonymous, *The German Spy*, trans. and ed. Thomas Lediard (London, 1738); Marquis d'Argen, *Chinese Letters* and *The Jewish Spy* (London,

1739). In addition to these, Montesquieu's *Persian Letters*
was translated into English in 1722, Eliza Haywood's *Letter
From the Palace of Fame* came out in 1727, and Goldsmith
continued the tradition in his *Letters From a Citizen of the
World* (1762).

27. Nicholas Breton, *A Poste with a Packet of Madde Letters*
(London, 1603), Preface.
28. G. P. Marana, *Letters Writ by a Turkish Spy*, trans. William
Bradshaw and Robert Midgeley, 6th ed. (London, 1694),
Preface.
29. Pierre Corlet de Chamblain Marivaux, *The Life of Marianne*
(London, 1736), Preface.
30. Robert Day, *Told in Letters*, p. 87. For a well-documented
case that fictions of all improbable sorts were accepted as
"histories," read Sidney I. Black's "Eighteenth-Century"
Histories' as a Fictional Mode," *Boston University English
Studies*, 1(1955), 38–44.
31. Daniel Defoe, *The Life and Strange Surprising Adventures
of Robinson Crusoe* (London, 1719), Introduction.
32. Eliza Haywood, *The Fair Hebrew: or, a True but Secret
History of Two Jewish Ladies who lately resided in London*
(London, 1729), Preface.
33. John Campbell, *The Polite Correspondence*, 3 vols.
(London, 1730?), I; reprinted in Natascha Würzbach, ed. *The
Novel in Letters* (Coral Gables, 1969), p. 187.
34. Aphra Behn, *Lycidus, or The Lover in Fashion* (London,
1688), p. 3.
35. *The Compleat Academy of Complements* (London, 1729),
Preface.
36. Mary Delariviere Manley, *Court Intrigues* (London, 1711),
Preface.
37. Thomas Sprat, *History of the Royal Society* (London, 1667),
p. 113. Reproduced by Washington University Studies (St.
Louis, Mo., 1958), ed. Jackson I. Cope and Harold Whitmore
Jones.
38. See, for example, Richard F. Jones, "Science and English
Prose Style in the Third Quarter of the 17th Century," *PMLA*
45(1930), 977–1009, or Marjorie Nicolson, "The Microscope
and the English Imagination," *Smith College Studies in
Modern Literature*, XVI:4(1935), 1–92.

39. Margaret Cavendish, *CCXI Sociable Letters* (London, 1664), Preface.

40. From a eulogizing letter from J. B. Freval, reprinted in Ioan W. Williams, ed., *Novel and Romance, 1700–1800: A Documentary Record* (London, 1970), p. 93.

41. Béat de Muralt, *Letters Describing the Character and Customs of the French and English Nations* (London, 1726), p. 83.

42. Pierre Corlet de Chamblain Marivaux, *The Life of Marianne*, p. 6.

43. *Ibid.*, Advertisement to Part II.

44. *Letters of Abelard and Héloise*, trans. John Hughes, 7th ed. (London, 1743), Preface.

45. Eliza Haywood, *The British Recluse* (London, 1722), p. 88.

46. Alexander Pope, *Letters*, I, xxxix–xl.

47. Defoe's *The Storm* is another letter collection created for a public which enjoyed an empirical cast to their reading. It is a collection of letters from people all over England—a sort of poll—about the effects of a terrible storm. There are reports of people being picked up and carried about by winds, of trees crashing down, of ships tossed about, etc.—all with a proper caution about facts:

> Tho' every circumstance in this Letter is not literally True, as to the Number of Ships, or Lives lost, and the Stile coarse, and Sailor like; yet I have inserted in this letter, because it seems to describe the Horror and consternation the poor sailors were in at that time.

There are poems occasioned by the storm and tables of barometric readings and even a letter from a trumped up Anthony van Lauwenhoek, F.R.S., written in lab report prose:

> Delft, January 8, 1704
> Upon the 8th of December, 1703 N.S. We had a dreadful Storm from the Southwest, insomuch, that the Water mingled with small parts of Chalk and Stone, was so dasht against the Glass-windows, that many of them were darkened therewith ... [and] ... deprived of most of their transparency.
> [Daniel Defoe, *The Storm* (London, 1704), p. 161.]

48. *The Night-Walker or Evening Rambles in Search after Lewd Women, with Conferences Held with Them* . . . ran from September 1696 to January 1697 and was dedicated to "the whoremasters of London and Westminster."

49. Philip Pinkus, *Grub Street Stripped Bare* (New York, 1968), p. 86.

50. Eliza Haywood, *Love-Letters on All Occasions Lately Passed Between Persons of Distiction* (London, 1730).
51. *Ibid.*, p. 128.
52. Samuel Richardson, *Letters Written To and For Particular Friends on the Most Important Occasions* (London, 1741), Letter LXII, p. 79.
53. *Ibid.*, Letter CXXXVIII.
54. Hannah Wolley, *The Gentlewoman's Companion; or A Guide to the Female Sex, with Letters and Discourses Upon All Occasions.* (London, 1673).
55. *The Diary of Dudley Ryder*, p. 164. Entry dated January 9, 1716.
56. Samuel Richardson, *Letters Written To and For Particular Friends on the Most Important Occasions*, pp. 13–16, 49–50, 160–161.

CHAPTER 4

Separation and Isolation in Epistolary Fiction

1. *The Unhappy Lovers or The Timorous Fair One*, authorship uncertain, possibly Mary Delariviere Manley (London, 1694), p. 10.
2. *Ibid.*, p. 30.
3. *The Illegal Lovers*, "Written by One who did reside in the Family" (London, 1728), p. 5.
4. *Ibid.*, p. 23.
5. *Ibid.*, p. 24.
6. Eliza Haywood, *Love-Letters on All Occasions Lately Passed Between Persons of Distinction* (London, 1730), p. 213.
7. *The Fatal Amour Between a Beautiful Lady and a Young Nobleman*, bound with *The Secret History of the Prince of the Nazarenes and Two Turks* (London, 1719).
8. See above, pp. 180–181, n. 26.
9. *The Spectator* No. 241, December 6, 1711.
10. Mary Delariviere Manley, *Court Intrigues, in a Collection of Original Letters From the Island of the New Atalantis* (London, 1711), p. 135.
11. George Farquhar, *Letters of Love and Business* (London, 1702), p. 81.

12. Eliza Haywood, *Some Memoirs of the Amours and Intrigues of a Certain Irish Dean* (London, 1728), p. 71.
13. Aphra Behn, *Love-Letters Between A Nobleman and His Sister* (London, 1694), Part I reprinted in Natascha Würzbach, *The Novel in Letters*, p. 223.
14. Mary Delariviere Manley, *Letters Written by Mrs. Manley* (London, 1713), pp. 85–86.
15. *Five Love-Letters From a Nun to a Cavalier*, trans. Roger L'Estrange (London, 1678), reprinted in Natascha Würzbach, *The Novel in Letters*, p. 62.
16. Franz Kafka, *Letter to His Father*, trans. Ernst Kaiser and Eithne Wilkins (New York, 1953), p. 125.
17. Mme. D'Aulnoy, *The Present Court of Spain*, trans. Thomas Brown (London, 1693), p. 262.
18. Aphra Behn, *Love-Letters Between A Nobleman and His Sister* (London, 1694), Part I reprinted in Natascha Würzbach, *The Novel in Letters*, p. 223.
19. Camilla writes this. Eliza Haywood, *Love in Excess* (London, 1719), Book III, p. 57.
20. *Five Love-Letters From a Nun to a Cavalier*, reprinted in Natascha Würzbach, *The Novel in Letters*, pp. 15–16.
21. Thomas D'Urfey, *Stories, Moral and Comical* (London, 1706), "The Prudent Husband," pp. 181–216.
22. *Letters of Abelard and Héloise*, trans. John Hughes (London, 1743), p. 134.
23. *Five Love-Letters From a Nun to a Cavalier*, reprinted in Natascha Würzbach, *The Novel in Letters*, p. 16.
24. *Five Love-Letters Written by a Cavalier in Answer to the Five Letters Written to Him by a Nun* (London, 1683), p. 44.
25. *The Adventures of Lindamira*, Revised and Corrected by Mr. Thomas Brown (London, 1702), p. 145.
26. *Five Love-Letters From a Nun to a Cavalier*, reprinted in Natascha Würzbach, *The Novel in Letters*, p. 11.
27. *Ibid.*, p. 21.
28. Soren Kierkegaard, *Repetition*, trans. Walter Lowrie (Princeton, N. J., 1941), p. 22.
29. *Ibid.*, p. 104.
30. *Ibid.*, p. 89.
31. *Letters of Abelard and Héloise*, p. 205.
32. *Ibid.*, pp. 149, 151.

33. *Five Love-Letters From a Nun to a Cavalier*, reprinted in Natascha Würzbach, *The Novel in Letters*, p. 21.
34. Natascha Würzbach, a historian of early epistolary fiction, noticing the effect of a too early marriage on one of these books, reports that "only the first book of *The Polite Correspondence* is interesting as a novel," and that the five other books which follow "suffer from the fact that after the two couples have been married off, nothing exciting happens." *The Novel in Letters*, p. 152.

CHAPTER 5

The Self As Word in Epistolary Fiction

1. James Boswell, *The Life of Samuel Johnson* (Oxford, 1953), p. 480.
2. Samuel Richardson, *The History of Sir Charles Grandison*, 7 vols. (London, 1753–1754), I, vi.
3. Prosper Crébillon, *fils, Letters From the Marchioness de M*** to the Count de R****, trans. Samuel Humphreys (London, 1735), Preface.
4. *Ibid.*, Letter XXII, p. 82; Letter XXIV, p. 90; Letter XXV, p. 94; Letter XXVI, p. 97; Letter XXIX, p. 111.
5. Mary Delariviere Manley, *The Secret History of Queen Zarah* (London, 1705), Preface.
6. Soren Kierkegaard, *Repetition*, trans. Walter Lowrie (Princeton, N. J., 1941), p. 135.
7. Marcel Proust, *Remembrance of Things Past*, trans. C. K. Moncrieff, 2 vols. (New York, 1934), I, 655.
8. Eliza Haywood, *Love-Letters on All Occasions Lately Passed Between Persons of Distinction* (London, 1730), p. 54. This seventy-five page sequence of letters between Theano and Elismonda (pp. 53–128) is the only story in this otherwise miscellaneous collection.
9. *Ibid.*, p. 58.
10. Prosper Crébillon, *fils, Letters From the Marchioness de M*** to the Count de R****, p. 103.
11. Aphra Behn, *Love-Letters Between A Nobleman and His Sister* (London, 1694), Part I reprinted in Natascha Würzbach, *The Novel in Letters*, p. 220.

12. Catherine Trotter, *Olinda's Adventures: or, The Amours of a Young Lady* appearing in *Familiar Letters of Love Gallantry and Several Other Occasions:* By the Wits of the Last and Present Age. Butler, Dryden, Congreve, Farquhar, etc. 2 vols. (London, 1724), II, 170. Italics added.
13. Mary Delariviere Manley, *Court Intrigues* (London, 1711), p. 138.
14. Mme. d'Aulnoy, *Memoires On The Court of England*, trans. C. J. (London, 1695), p. 376.
15. *Ibid.*, p. 373.
16. *Ibid.*, p. 376.
17. *Ibid.*, p. 392.
18. *Ibid.*, p. 392.
19. Choderlos de Laclos, *Les Liaisons dangereuses*, trans. Richard Aldington (New York, 1962), pp. 341–342.
20. By 1743 there had been seven editions of these letters in England, besides pirated printings.
21. *The Letters of Héloise and Abelard*, trans. John Hughes (London, 1743), pp. 115–117. The letter also appears in a translation by Roger L'Estrange in *Familiar Letters of Love Gallantry and Several Other Occasions:* By the Wits of the last and present age. Butler, Dryden, Congreve, Farquhar, etc. 2 vols., I, 223.
22. Sigmund Freud, "The Taboo on Virginity" (1918), reprinted in *On Creativity and the Unconscious*, ed. Benjamin Nelson (New York, 1958), p. 187.
23. See *The French Convert*, trans. Charles Gildon (London, 1701); Jane Barker, *The Lining of the Patch-work Screen* (London, 1726); Eliza Haywood, *The Agreeable Caledonian* (London, 1728); Eliza Haywood, *Love in Excess* (London, 1719).
24. Not surprisingly, heroines are Protestant in English novels.
25. George Farquhar, *Letters of Love and Business* (London, 1702), p. 55.
26. Mary Davys, "Familiar Letters Betwixt a Gentleman and a Lady" in *The Works of Mrs. Davys*, 2 vols. (London, 1725), II, 268.
27. Eliza Haywood, *Love in Excess* (London, 1719).
28. Hannah Wolley, *The Gentlewoman's Companion* (London, 1673), p. 234.

29. Eliza Haywood, *The Agreeable Caledonian* (London, 1728).
30. Eliza Haywood, *The British Recluse* (London, 1722), p. 42.
31. Anonymous [John Campbell?], *The Polite Correspondence: or Rational Amusement* (London, 1730 ?).

CHAPTER 6

Romantic Love and Sexual Fantasy in Epistolary Fiction

1. *The Adventures of Lindamira,* Revised and Corrected by Mr. Thomas Brown (London, 1702), p. 2.
2. *The Spectator,* No. 479, September 9, 1712.
3. *The Complete Letters of Lady Mary Wortley Montagu,* ed. Robert Halsband, 3 vols. (Oxford, 1965), III, 8–9. Letter to Lady Bute, March 1, 1752.
4. *Ibid.,* I, 123n. Mandane is the runaway heroine of Madelaine de Scudéry's *Artamène ou le Grand Cyrus* (1649–1653), which Lady Mary read as early as 1705.
5. *Ibid.,* I, 133–134.
6. *Ibid.,* I, 149–150. The exact date of this letter is unknown. Phillipa Mundy was a close friend of Lady Mary's age: she was Lady Mary's "Anna Howe."
7. *Ibid.,* I, 163–164. In the heat of this excitement, Lady Mary was writing Wortley twice a day: two letters on August 15, two letters on August 16, and an earlier one on August 17 precede this letter. Weary students of epistolary fiction should take note that people *did* write an extraordinary number of letters.
8. *Ibid.,* I, 164.
9. *Ibid.,* I, 164.
10. *Ibid.,* III, 9. Letter to Lady Bute, March 1, 1752.
11. Samuel Richardson, *Clarissa,* 4 vols. (London, 1748), I, 186.
12. *The Diary of Samuel Pepys,* ed. Henry B. Wheatley, 2 vols. (New York, 1893), I, 513–514. Entry dated November 13, 1662.
13. *The Complete Letters of Lady Mary Wortley Montagu,* ed. Robert Halsband, I, 175. Letter to Wortley, December 8, 1712.
14. *The Tatler,* No. 248, November 8, 1710.

15. Philippe Ariès, *Centuries of Childhood,* trans. Robert Baldick (New York, 1962) pp. 349–350 and *passim.* Lawrence Stone disagrees about the evidence of children's dress styles, but generally supports Ariès' conclusions that England was moving towards a more child-oriented society. Lawrence Stone, *The Family, Sex, and Marriage* (New York, 1977), pp. 405–449.

16. Mary Astell, *The Christian Religion as Profess'd by a Daughter of the Church of England* (London, 1705), pp. 292–293.

17. Choderlos de Laclos, *Les Liaisons dangereuses.* trans. Richard Addington (New York, 1962), p. 178.

18. *Five Love-Letters From a Nun to a Cavalier,* trans. Roger L'Estrange (London, 1678), reprinted in Natascha Würzbach, *The Novel in Letters,* p. 19.

19. "The Lady's New Year Gift, or Advice to a Daughter," *The Life and Letters of Sir George Saville, Bart. First Marquis of Halifax,* 2 vols. ed. H. C. Foxcroft (London, 1898), II, 410.

20. *Ibid.,* II, 408.

21. *The Spectator,* No. 66, May 16, 1711.

22. *Ibid.*

23. Anonymous [possibly Judith Drake], *A Farther Essay Relating to the Female Sex* (London, 1696), p. 59.

24. Anonymous [possibly Mrs. Steele], *The Ladies Library,* 3 vols. (London, 1714), III, 90.

25. Béat de Muralt, *Letters Describing the Character and Customs of the English and French Nations* (London, 1726), p. 35.

26. Philogamous, *The Present State of Matrimony* (London, 1739), p. 67.

27. Ruth Kelso, *Doctrine for the Lady of the Renaissance* (Urbana, 1965), p. 105.

28. *The Spectator,* No. 611, October 24, 1714.

29. Peter Laslett dates the use of contraceptive devices to Geneva at the end of the seventeenth century. *The World We Have Lost* (New York, 1965), p. 132.

30. T. C. Surgeon, *The Charitable Surgeon* (London, 1708), p. 58.

31. *The Tatler,* No. 15, May 13, 1709.

32. Daniel Defoe, *Conjugal Lewdness* (London, 1727), p. 132.

33. Mary Delariviere Manley, *Court Intrigues* (London, 1711), p. 138.
34. *The Letters of Abelard and Héloise*, trans. John Hughes (London, 1743), p. 185.
35. Eliza Haywood, *Love in Excess* (London, 1719), Part II, 47.
36. *Ibid.*
37. Jane Barker, *The Lining to the Patch-work Screen* (London, 1726), p. 106.
38. Anonymous [possibly Mrs. Steele], *The Ladies Library*, II, 46.
39. Eliza Haywood, *Love in Excess*, p. 36.
40. Charles Gildon, *The Post-Boy Rob'd of His Mail* (London, 1692), p. 237.
41. Mary Delariviere Manley, "From a Lady To a Lady," Letter XXXIII in *Court Intrigues* (London, 1711), reprinted in Natascha Würzbach, *The Novel in Letters*, p. 44.
42. Mary Delariviere Manley, *Secret Memoirs and Manners of Several Persons of Quality of Both Sexes From New Atalantis* (London, 1709), p. 67.
43. Mary Delariviere Manley, *Rivella*, p. 4, bound with *Court Intrigues* (London, 1711).
44. Aphra Behn, *Love-Letters Between A Nobleman and His Sister* (London, 1694), reprinted in Natascha Würzbach, *The Novel in Letters*, p. 246.
45. Mary Delariviere Manley, *Court Intrigues*, p. 36.
46. Eliza Haywood, *Love-Letters on All Occasions* (London, 1730), p. 103.
47. Aphra Behn, *Love-Letters Between A Nobleman and His Sister*, reprinted in Natascha Würzbach, *The Novel in Letters*, p. 230.
48. Mary Delariviere Manley, *Court Intrigues*, p. 36.
49. *The Dairy of Samuel Pepys*, II, 768–769. Entry dated January 13, 1668.
50. *Ibid.*, II, 790. Entry dated February 8, 1668.
51. *Ibid.*, II, 790.
52. David Foxon, *Libertine Literature in England, 1660–1745* (New York, 1965) p. 48.
53. "The Dancing School," *A Collection of the Writings of Mr. Edward Ward*, 6 vols. (London, 1717–1718), II, 237.
54. Mary Davys, "Familiar Letters Betwixt a Gentleman and a

Lady", *The Works of Mrs. Davys*, 2 vols. (London, 1725), II, 299.

55. Anonymous, *The Unnatural Mother and Ungrateful Wife* (London, 1730), p. 11.

56. René Girard, *Deceit, Desire, and the Novel* (Baltimore, 1965), Chapter 1.

57. Anna Letitia Barbauld, "Richardson," *The British Novelists*, 50 vols. (London, 1810), I, xiv. Barbauld, besides being a great admirer of Richardson's technique, was the first editor of *his* letters.

58. Samuel Richardson, *Pamela, or Virtue Rewarded*, 2nd edition (London, 1741), Introduction, pp. xxiv–xxv.

Bibliography

EPISTOLARY FICTION CITED

Abelard and Héloise. *Letters of Abelard and Héloise*. trans. John Hughes. 7th edn. London, 1743.

Addison, Joseph, Sir Richard Steele, *et al. The Spectator*. London, March, 1711—December, 1712; June–September, 1714.

Anonymous. *Atterburyana*. London, 1727.

Anonymous. *The Double Captive or Chains Upon Chains*. London, 1718.

Anonymous. *The Fatal Amour Between a Beautiful Lady and a Young Nobleman* bound with *The Secret History of The Nazarenes and Two Turks*. London, 1719.

Anonymous. *Five Love-Letters From a Nun to a Cavalier*. trans. Roger L'Estrange. London, 1678.

Anonymous. *Five Love-Letters Written by a Cavalier in Answer to the Five Letters Written to Him by a Nun*. London, 1683.

Anonymous. *The French Convert*. trans. Charles Gildon. London, 1701.

Anonymous. *The Gentleman Apothecary*. London, 1678.

Anonymous. *The German Spy*. trans. and ed. Thomas Lediard. London, 1738.

Anonymous. *The Illegal Lovers*. London, 1728.

Anonymous. *Love-Letters Between Polydorus, The Gothick King and Messalina, Late Queen of Albion*. London, 1689.

Anonymous. *Perfidious P.* London, 1702.

Anonymous. *The Unnatural Mother and Ungrateful Wife.* London, 1730 [date uncertain].

Barker, Jane. *The Lining to the Patch-Work Screen.* London, 1726.

Barker, Jane. *A Patch-Work Screen For The Ladies.* London, 1723.

Behn, Aphra. *Love-Letters Between A Nobleman and His Sister.* London, 1694.

Behn, Aphra. *Lycidus: Or The Lover in Fashion.* Being An Account from Lycidus to Lysander, of his voyage from the Island of Love. From the French. London, 1688.

Behn, Aphra. *The Works of Aphra Behn.* 6 vols. ed. Montague Summers. London: W. Heinemann, 1915.

Boyer, Abel. "Captain Ayloffe's Letters" in *Letters of Wit, Politics and Morality.* London, 1701.

Breton, Nicholas. *A Poste with a Packet of Madde Letters.* London, 1603.

Brown, Thomas [authorship uncertain]. *The Adventures of Lindamira.* Revised and Corrected. London, 1702.

Brown, Thomas. *Familiar Letters of Love, Gallantry and Several Other Occasions:* By the Wits of the Last and Present Age: Butler, Dryden, Congreve, Farquhar, etc. 2 vols. London, 1724.

Brown, Thomas. *Letters From the Dead to the Living* by Thomas Brown, Captain Ayloffe, and Mr. Henry Barker. London, 1702.

Brown, Thomas. *Letters from The Dead, A Continuation Or Second Part of the Letters from the Dead to the Living.* By Mr. Thomas Brown, Captain Ayloffe, and Mr. Henry Barker. London, 1703.

Brown, Thomas. *The Works of Mr. Thomas Brown.* 2 vols. London, 1707.

Campbell, John [authorship uncertain]. *The Polite Correspondence.* 3 vols. London, 1730, [date uncertain].

Crébillon, Prosper, *fils. Letters From The Marchioness de M*** to the Count de R***.* trans. from the original French by Mr. Humphreys. London, 1735.

D'Argen, Marquis. *Chinese Letters.* trans. anon. London, 1739.

D'Argen, Marquis. *The Jewish Spy.* trans. anon. London, 1739.

D'Aulnoy, Mme. *Memoires On The Court of England.* trans. C. J. London, 1695.

D'Aulnoy, Mme. *The Present Court of Spain.* trans. Thomas Brown. London, 1693.

Davys, Mary. "Familiar Letters Betwixt a Gentleman and a Lady". *The Works of Mrs. Davys.* 2 vols. London, 1725, II; also available ed. and intro. by Robert A. Day, Los Angeles: William Andrews Clark Memorial Library, University of California, 1955.

Defoe, Daniel. *A Continuation of Letters Writ By A Turkish Spy at Paris.* London, 1718.

Defoe, Daniel. *Letters From the Living to the Living.* London, 1703.

Defoe, Daniel. *The Storm.* London, 1704.

De Fontenelle, Bernard Le Bovier. *Letters of Gallantry.* trans. Mr. Ozell. London, 1715.

Du Noyer, Mme. Anne Marguerite Petit. *Letters from a Lady at Paris to a Lady at Avignon.* London, 1716.

Dunton, John. *The Athenian Spy.* London, 1704.

D'Urfey, Thomas. *Stories Moral and Comical.* London, 1706.

Farquhar, George. *Letters of Love and Business.* London, 1702.

Gildon, Charles. *Letters and Essays on several subjects: Philosophical, Moral, Historical, Critical, Amorous, etc. in Prose and Verse.* London, 1697.

Gildon, Charles. *The Post-Boy Rob'd of His Mail.* London, 1692.

Haywood, Eliza. *The Agreeable Caledonian.* London, 1728.

Haywood, Eliza. *The British Recluse.* London, 1722.

Haywood, Eliza. *The Disguis'd Prince or, The Beautiful Parisian.* London, 1726.

Haywood, Eliza. *The Fair Hebrew: or, a True but Secret History of Two Jewish Ladies who lately resided in London.* London, 1729.

Haywood, Eliza. *The Fatal Secret, or Constancy in Distress.* London, 1724.

Haywood, Eliza. *The Injured Husband.* London, 1724.

Haywood, Eliza. *Irish Artifice; or, The History of Clarina.* London, 1728.

Haywood, Eliza. *Letter From the Palace of Fame.* 1727.

Haywood, Eliza. *Letters From a Lady of Quality to a Cavalier.* London, 1724.

Haywood, Eliza. *Letter From a Lady of Quality to a Chevalier.* London, 1724.

Haywood, Eliza. *Love in Excess; or The Fatal Enquiry.* London, 1719.

Haywood, Eliza. "The Distress'd Beauty", Good out of Evil", "Female Revenge", "Love Pos'd", "The Hasty Marriage", "The Witty Reclaimer". *Love in Its Variety; Being a Collection of Select Novels written in Spanish by Signior Michael Bandello.* London, 1727.

Haywood, Eliza. *Love-Letters on All Occasions Lately Passed Between Persons of Distinction.* London, 1730.

Haywood, Eliza. *Memoirs of a Certain Island.* London, 1725.

Haywood, Eliza. *Persecuted Virtue.* London, 1729.

Haywood, Eliza. *Some Memoirs of the Amours and Intrigues of a Certain Irish Dean.* London, 1728.

Haywood, Eliza. *A Spy Upon The Conjurer.* [sometimes attributed to Defoe]. London, 1724.

Laclos, Choderlos de. *Les Liaisons dangereuses.* trans. Richard Aldington. New York: New American Library, 1962.

Manley, Mary Delariviere. *Court Intrigues in a Collection of Original Letters from the Island of the New Atalantis* [Including "From A Lady To A Lady"]. London, 1711.

Manley, Mary Delariviere. *A Lady's Packet of Letters Broke Open.* London, 1707.

Manley, Mary Delariviere. *Letters Written by Mrs. Manley.* London, 1713.

Manley, Mary Delariviere. "The Fair Hypocrite", "The Physician's Strategem", "The Wife's Resentment", "The Husband's Resentment in Two Examples", "The Happy Fugitives", "The Perjur'd Beauty". *The Power of Love.* London, 1720.

Manley, Mary Delariviere. *The Secret History of Queen Zarah.* London, 1705.

Manley, Mary Delariviere. *Secret Memoirs and Manners of Several Persons of Quality of Both Sexes From New Atalantis.* London, 1709.

Manley, Mary Delariviere [authorship uncertain]. *The Unhappy Lovers or The Timorous Fair One.* London, 1694.

Marana, G. P. *Letters Writ By A Turkish Spy.* 8 vols. trans. William Bradshaw and Robert Midgeley. London, 1687-1694.

Marivaux, Pierre Corlet de Chamblain. *The Life of Marianne.* London, 1736.

Marten, Col. Henry. *Familiar Letters to His Lady of Delight: also Her Kinde Returnes.* London, 1662.

Montesquieu, Charles de Secondat. *Persian Letters.* trans. Mr. Ozell. London, 1722.

Ratisbone, L. S. *An Account of the Secret Services of M. de Vernay.* Amsterdam, 1683.

Richardson, Samuel. *Clarissa, or History of a Young Lady.* 4 vols. London, 1747–1748.

Richardson, Samuel. *The History of Sir Charles Grandison.* 7 vols. London, 1753–1754.

Richardson, Samuel. *Letters Written To and For Particular Friends on the Most Important Occasions.* London, 1741.

Richardson, Samuel. *Pamela, or Virtue Rewarded.* London, 1741.

Rousseau, Jean Jacques. *La Nouvelle Heloise ou Lettres de deux amans, habitans d'une petite ville au pied des Alpes; recueilies et publiées par Jean Jacques Rousseau.* Paris, 1781.

Trotter, Mrs. Catherine. *Olinda's Adventures: or, The Amours of a Young Lady,* originally published 1693, reprinted in *Familiar Letters of Love, Gallantry and Several Other Occasions by the Wits of the Last and Present Age: Butler, Dryden, Congreve, Farquhar, etc.* 2 vols. London, 1724, II, 121–186.

Ward, Edward. *A New Voyage to the Island of Fools.* London, 1715.

Ward, Edward. "A Paquet From Will's." in *The Second Volume of the Works of Monsieur Voiture.* London, 1705.

Ward, Edward. *A Trip to Jamaica.* London, 1698.

Ward, Edward. *A Trip to New England,* London, 1699, bound with *Letter From New England Concerning Their Customs, Manners, and Religion.* reprinted by the Club for Colonial Reprints. ed. George Parker Winship. Providence, 1905.

PRIMARY SOURCES

Anonymous. *The Brothers, or Treachery Punish'd.* "By A Person of Quality." London, 1730.

Anonymous. *The Cabinet Opened, or The Secret History of the Amours of Madame de Maintenon.* London, 1690.

Anonymous. *The Compleat Academy of Complements.* London, 1729.

Anonymous. [possibly written by Judith Drake]. *A Farther Essay Relating to the Female Sex.* London, 1696.

Anonymous. *The Friendly Society for Widows: being a Proposal for Supplying the Defect of Joyntures and Securing Women from falling into Poverty and Distress at the Deaths of Their Husbands.* London, 1696.

Anonymous. *A Letter from a By-Stander, containing Remarks on and Objections to the Bill now depending in Parliament, for the better Preventing Clandestine Marriages.* London, 1753.

Anonymous. *Marriage Promoted: In a Discourse of Its Ancient and Modern Practice both under Heathen and Christian Commonwealths.* London, 1690.

Anonymous. *The Masqueraders, or Fatal Curiosity.* London, 1724.

Anonymous. "A New Method for making Women as useful and as capable of maintaining themselves as the Men are; and consequently preventing them becoming Old Maids or taking ill courses." *Gentleman's Magazine.* vol. 9 (1739), p. 525.

Anonymous. *The Penitant Hermit, or The Fruits of Jealousy.* London, 1679.

Anonymous. *The Player's Tragedy, or Fatal Love.* London, 1693.

Anonymous. *The Present State of Matrimony.* by Philogamus. London, 1739.

Astell, Mary. *The Christian Religion as Profess'd by a Daughter of The Church of England.* London, 1705.

Astell, Mary. *A Serious Proposal to the Ladies For the Advancement of Their True and Greatest Interest.* London, 1694.

Astell, Mary. *Some Reflections Upon Marriage.* London, 1700.

Austen, Jane. *Persuasion.* London, 1818.

Black, William. *Observations Medical and Political on the Small Pox and the Mortality of Mankind at Every Age in City and Country.* London, 1781.

Boswell, James. *The Life of Samuel Johnson.* Oxford: Oxford University Press, 1953.

Boyd, Elizabeth. *The Happy Unfortunate; or, The Female Page.* London, 1732.

Browning, Andrew, ed. *English Historical Documents, 1660-1714.* vol. VIII. London: Eyre & Spottiswoode, 1953.

Burney, Frances. *Cecilia: or Memoirs of an Heiress.* 5 vols. London, 1782.

Burney, Frances. *Evelina: or The History of a Young Lady's Entrance into the World.* 3 vols. London, 1778.

Cavendish, Margaret, Duchess of Newcastle. *CCXI Sociable Letters.* London, 1664.

Curll, Edmund. *Letters, Poems, and Tales: Amorous, Satyrical and Gallant which passed between Several Persons of Distinction.* London, 1718.

Defoe, Daniel. *The Compleat English Gentleman.* London, 1730.

Defoe, Daniel. *Conjugal Lewdness: or Matrimonial Whoredom.* London, 1727.

Defoe, Daniel. *The Earlier Life and the Chief Earlier Works of Daniel Defoe.* ed. Henry Morley. London: Routledge, 1889.

Defoe, Daniel. *Essay on Projects.* London, 1697.

Defoe, Daniel. *Everybody's Business Nobody's Business.* London, 1725.

Defoe, Daniel. *The Family Instructor.* London, 1715.

Defoe, Daniel. *The Life and Strange Surprising Adventures of Robinson Crusoe.* London, 1719.

Defoe, Daniel. *Moll Flanders.* ed. James Sutherland. Boston: Houghton Mifflin Co., 1959.

Defoe, Daniel. *A Tour Thro' The Whole Island of Great Britain.* 3 vols. London, 1726, reprinted in a limited edition with an introduction by G.D.H. Cole. London: Peter Davies, 1927.

De Muralt, Béat. *Letters Describing the Character and Customs of the French and English Nations.* London, 1726.

De Saussure, Cesar. *Lettres et Voyages.* Laussane, 1903.

Dunton, John. *The Athenian Gazette.* London, March, 1690—February, 1696.

Dunton, John. *The Female Warr.* London, c. 1690.

Dunton, John. *The Night-Walker, or Evening Rambles in Search after Lewd Women, with Conferences Held with Them.* London, September 1696 to January 1697.

Evelyn, John. *The Diary of John Evelyn*. ed. E. S. de Beer. London: Oxford University Press, 1959.

Fielding, Henry. *The History of Tom Jones*. London, 1749.

Haywood, Eliza. *Fantomina: or Love in a Maze*. London, 1725.

Haywood, Eliza. *The Rash Resolve*, in *The Works of Mrs. Eliza Haywood*. 4 vols. London, 1724.

Kalm, Pehr. *Pehr Kalm's Account of His Visit to England (1748)*. trans. Joseph Lucas. London: Macmillan, 1892.

L'Estrange, Roger. *Brief History of the Times*. London, 1687.

Long, Mrs. Anne. *Letters, Poems, and Tales from the Cabinet of Mrs. Anne Long*. London, 1718.

Maitland, W. *A History and Survey of London*. London, 1739.

Marten, John. *A Treatise Of all the Degrees and Symptoms of the Venereal Disease, In both Sexes*. Sixth Edition. London, 1708.

Mission, M. *Memoirs and Observations in His Travels Over England*. trans. Ozell. London, 1718.

Montagu, Lady Mary Wortley. *The Complete Letters of Lady Mary Wortley Montagu*. 3 vols. ed. Robert Halsband. Oxford: Clarendon Press, 1965.

Nichols, David. *The Correspondence of Dean Atterbury*. 5 vols. London, 1783–1790.

Pepys, Samuel. *The Diary of Samuel Pepys*. 2 vols. ed. Henry B. Wheatley. London: G. Bell & Sons, 1893.

Pope, Alexander. *Correspondence of Alexander Pope*. 5 vols. ed. George Sherburn. Oxford: Clarendon Press, 1956.

Royal Society. *Philosophical Transactions*. London, 1665—.

Ryder, Dudley. *The Diary of Dudley Ryder*. ed. William Mathews. London, 1939.

Salmon, Thomas. *A Critical Essay Concerning Marriage*. London, 1724.

Saville, Sir George. "The Lady's New Year's Gift or Advice to a Daughter." *The Life and Letters of Sir George Saville, Bart. First Marquis of Halifax*. 2 vols. ed. H. C. Foxcroft. London: Longmans, 1898, II, pp. 388–424.

Sprat, Thomas. *History of the Royal Society*. London, 1667. ed. Jackson I. Cope and Harold Whitmore Jones, St. Louis, Missouri: Washington University Studies, 1958.

Stanhope, Philip Dormer. *The Letters of Philip Dormer Stanhope, IV Earl of Chesterfield*. 6 vols. ed. Bonamy Dobrée. New York: Viking Press, 1932, II.

Steele, Mrs. [authorship uncertain]. *The Ladies Library.* 3 vols. London, 1714.

Steele, Sir Richard, Joseph Addison, *et al. The Guardian.* London, "By Nestor Ironside," *[pseud.]* London, March—October, 1713.

Steele, Sir Richard, Joseph Addison, *et al. The Tatler.* "By Isaac Bickerstaffe," *[pseud.]* London, April, 1709—January, 1711.

Surgeon, T. C. *[pseud.] The Charitable Surgeon.* London, 1708. [Probably a pirated edition of John Marten's *A Treatise Of all the Degrees and Symptoms*. . . .]

Swift, Jonathan. *"Gulliver's Travels" and Other Writings.* ed. Louis A. Landa. Boston: Houghton Mifflin Co., 1960.

Swift, Jonathan. *Miscellaneous and Autobiographical Pieces, Fragments, and Marginalia.* ed. Herbert Davis and Basil Blackwell. Oxford: Blackwell, 1962.

Swift, Jonathan. "A Letter to a Young Lady on Her Marriage." *Satires and Personal Writings by Jonathan Swift.* ed. William Alfred Eddy. London and New York: Oxford University Press, 1932, pp. 59–72.

Ward, Edward. *The Batchelor's Estimate of the Expenses of a Married Life.* London, 1725.

Ward, Edward. *A Collection of the Writings of Mr. Edward Ward.* 2 vols. London, 1717–1718.

Ward, Edward. *Female Policy Detected: or The Arts of a Designing Woman Laid Open.* London, 1695.

Ward, Edward. *Marriage-Dialogues: or A Poetical Peep into the State of Matrimony.* London, 1708.

Wheler, George. *A Protestant Monastery.* London, 1698.

Williams, Ioan W. *Novel and Romance, 1700-1800: a Documentary Record.* London: Routledge, 1970.

Wolley, Hannah. *The Gentlewoman's Companion; or a Guide to the Female Sex, with Letters and Discourses Upon All Ocasions.* London, 1673.

SECONDARY SOURCES

Alexander, William. *A History of Women.* 2 vols. 3rd edn. London, 1782.

Aries, Philippe. *Centuries of Childhood.* trans. Robert Baldick. New York: Random House, 1962.

Ashton, John. *Social Life in the Reign of Queen Anne.* London: Chatto & Windus, 1897.

Baker, Ernest A., *The History of the English Novel.* 8 vols. London: Witherby, 1938.

Barbauld, Anna Letitia, ed. *The British Novelists.* 50 vols. London, 1810.

Beard, Mary. *On Understanding Women.* London: Longmans, Green, and Co., 1931.

Beard, Mary. *Woman as A Force in History.* New York: The Macmillan Co., 1946.

Black, Frank Gees. *The Epistolary Novel in the Late Eighteenth Century.* Eugene, Oregon: University of Oregon Press, 1940.

Black, Sidney J. "Eighteenth Century 'Histories' as a Fictional Mode." *Boston University Studies in English,* I(1955), pp. 38–44.

Blease, Lyon Walter. *The Emancipation of English Women.* London: D. Nutt, 1913.

Boyce, Benjamin. *Tom Brown of Facetious Memory.* Vol. XXI of *Harvard Studies in English.* Cambridge, Mass.: Harvard University Press, 1939.

Browning, Andrew, ed. *English Historical Documents, 1660–1714.* Vol. VIII. London: Eyre & Spottiswoode, 1953.

Cassirer, Ernst. *The Philosophy of the Enlightenment.* trans. Fritz C. Koelln and James P. Pettegrove. Princeton: Princeton University Press, 1951.

Chapman, R. W. "The Course of the Post in the Eighteenth Century." *Notes and Queries,* 183(1942), pp. 67–69.

Clark, Alice. *Working Life of Women in the Seventeenth Century.* London: G. Routledge & Sons, Ltd., 1919.

Cole, Margaret. *Marriage: Past and Present.* London: J. M. Dent & Sons Ltd., 1938.

Collins, A. S. "The Growth of the Reading Public During the Eighteenth Century." *Review of English Studies,* II(1926), pp. 284–294, 428–438.

Day, Robert Adams. *Told in Letters.* Ann Arbor: University of Michigan Press, 1966.

Ehrenreich, Barbara, and Deirdre English. *Witches, Midwives and Nurses, A History of Women Healers.* Old Westbury: The Feminist Press, 1973.

Fiedler, Leslie. *Love and Death in the American Novel.* New York: Stein and Day, 1966.

Ford, Boris. ed. *From Dryden to Johnson.* Vol. 4 of *The Pelican Guide to English Literature.* Baltimore: Penguin Books, Inc., 1957.

Foucault, Michael. *Madness and Civilization.* trans. Richard Howard. New York: New American Library, 1965.

Foxon, David. *Libertine Literature in England, 1660–1745.* New York: University Books, 1965.

Frank, Joseph. *The Beginnings of the English Newspaper, 1620–1660.* Cambridge, Mass.: Harvard University Press, 1961.

Freud, Sigmund. "The Taboo on Virginity" (1918). reprinted in *On Creativity and the Unconscious.* ed. Benjamin Nelson. New York: Harper & Row, 1958.

Fryer, Peter. *The Birth Controllers.* London: Secker & Warburg, 1965.

George, M. Dorothy. *England in Transition.* London: G. Routledge & Sons, Ltd., 1931.

George, M. Dorothy. *London Life in the Eighteenth Century.* New York: Harper & Row. 1964.

Girard, René. *Deceit, Desire, and The Novel.* Baltimore: Johns Hopkins University Press, 1965.

Glass, D. V. and D. E. C. Eversley. *Population in History: Essays in Historical Demography.* London: Edward Arnold, 1965.

Goodman, Paul. *Structures of Literature.* Chicago: University of Chicago Press, 1954.

Habakkuk, H. J. "Marriage Settlements in the 18th Century." *Transactions of the Royal Society.* 4th Series, XXXII(1950), pp. 15–30.

Hill, Christopher. *Puritanism and Revolution.* London: Secker & Warburg and New York: Schocken Books, 1958.

Hill, Christopher. *Socity and Puritanism in Pre-Revolutionary England.* London: Secker & Warburg and New York: Schocken Books, 1964.

Horn, D. B., and Mary Ransome. eds. *English Historical Documents, 1714–1783*. Vol. X. London: Eyre & Spottiswoode, 1957.

Horner, Joyce M. *The English Women Novelists and Their Connection with the Feminist Movement (1699–1797)*. Vol. XI, Nos. 1,2,3, of *Smith College Studies in Modern Languages*. Northampton, Mass.: The Collegiate Press, 1929–1930.

Irving, William Henry. *The Providence of Wit in The English Letter-Writers*. Durham: Duke University Press, 1955.

Jones, Richard F. "Science and English Prose Style in the Third Quarter of the 17th Century." *PMLA*, 45(1930), pp. 977–1009.

Kafka, Franz. *Letter to His Father*. trans. Ernst Kaiser and Eithne Wilkins. New York: Schocken Books, 1953.

Kamm, Josephine. *Hope Deferred*. London: Methuen, 1965.

Kelso, Ruth. *Doctrine for The Lady of the Renaissance*. Urbana: University of Illinois Press, 1965.

Kierkegaard, Soren. *Repetition*. trans. Walter Lowrie. Princeton: Princeton University Press, 1941.

Laslett, Peter. *The World We Have Lost*. New York: Charles Scribner's Sons, 1965.

Leavis, Q. D. *Fiction and the Reading Public*. London: Chatto & Windus, 1932.

Lowenthal, Leo and Marjorie Fiske: "The English Eighteenth Century As a Case Study," in *Literature, Popular Culture and Society*. ed. Leo Lowenthal. Englewood Cliffs, New Jersey: Prentice-Hall, 1961, pp. 52–108.

MacCarthy, B. G. *Women Writers, Their Contribution to the English Novel 1621–1744*. Oxford: Blackwell, Ltd., 1944.

McBurney, William M. *A Checklist of Prose Fiction 1700–1739*. Cambridge, Mass.: Harvard University Press, 1960.

McBurney, William M. "Edmund Curll, Mrs. Jane Barker, and The English Novel." *Philological Quarterly*, XXXVII, No. 4(1958), pp. 385–399.

Marx, Karl. *The German Ideology, 1845–46*. trans. 1965. New York: International Publishers, 1965.

Mayo, Robert. *The English Novel in the Magazines 1740–1815*. Evanston: Northwestern University Press, 1962.

Mish, Charles C. *English Prose Fiction, 1600–1700, A Chronological Checklist.* Charlottesville, Virginia: Bibliographical Society of the University of Virginia, 1967.

Mumford, Lewis. *The City In History.* New York: Harcourt Brace & World, 1961.

Newton, John. *Women's Position Before English Law, from Anglo-Saxon Times Until Today.* London: Stevens & Sons, 1899.

Nicolson, Marjorie. "The Microscope and The English Imagination." *Smith College Studies in Modern Literature,* XVI, No. 4(1935), pp. 1–92.

Nicolson, Marjorie and Nora Mohler. "The Scientific Background of Swift's Voyage to Laputa." *Annals of Science,* II(1937), pp. 299–334.

O'Malley, Ida Beatrice. *Women in Subjection, A Study of The Lives of Englishwomen before 1832.* London: Duckworth, 1933.

Owen, David. *English Philanthropy, 1660–1960.* Cambridge, Mass.: Harvard University Press, 1964.

Paulson, Ronald. *Hogarth: His Life, Art and Times.* 2 vols. New Haven: Yale University Press, 1971.

Phillips, M. and W. S. Tompkinson. *English Women in Life and Letters.* Oxford: Oxford University Press, 1926.

Pinchbeck, Ivy. *Women Workers in the Industrial Revolution, 1750–1850.* London: G. Routledge & Sons, 1930.

Pinkus, Philip. *Grub Street Stripped Bare.* Hamden, Conn.: Archon Books, 1968.

Plumb, J. H. *England in the Eighteenth Century.* Harmondsworth, Middlesex: Penguin Books, 1950.

Poole, Austin Lane. *Obligations of Society in the Twelfth and Thirteenth Centuries.* Oxford: Oxford University Press, 1946.

Power, Eileen. *Medieval Women.* Cambridge: Cambridge University Press, 1975.

Preston, John. *The Created Self; The Reader's Role in Eighteenth Century Fiction.* London: Heinemann, 1970.

Proust, Marcel. *Remembrance of Things Past.* trans. C. K. Moncrieff. 2 vols. New York: Random House, 1934.

Reynolds, Myra. *The Learned Lady in England, 1650–1760.* Boston: Houghton Mifflin Co., 1920.

Richards, Eric. "Women in the British Economy Since About 1700: An Interpretation." *History,* 59(1974), pp. 337–357.

Richetti, John J. *Popular Fiction Before Richardson: Narrative Patterns 1700–1739.* Oxford: Clarendon Press, 1969.

Rowbotham, Sheila. *Women, Resistance and Revolution.* London: A. Lane, 1972.

Shorter, Edward. *The Making of the Modern Family.* New York: Basic Books, 1975.

Singer, Godfrey Frank. *The Epistolary Novel.* New York: Russell & Russell, 1963.

Slater, M. "The Weightiest Business: Marriage in an Upper-Gentry Family in Seventeenth-Century England." *Past and Present,* 72(August, 1976), pp. 25–55.

Souers, Philip Webster. *The Matchless Orinda.* Vol. V of *Harvard Studies In English.* Cambridge, Mass.: Harvard University Press, 1931.

Spector, Robert Donald, ed. *Essays on the Eighteenth-Century Novel.* Bloomington: University of Indiana Press, 1965.

Starr, George A. *Defoe and Spiritual Autobiography.* Princeton: Princeton University Press, 1965.

Stauffer, Ruth. "The Relation of Women to English Literature from 1558 to 1660." Unpublished Thesis. Radcliffe College, 1942.

Stenton, Doris Mary. *The English Woman in History.* London: Allen & Unwin, 1957.

Stephen, Leslie. *English Literature and Society in the Eighteenth Century.* London: Duckworth & Company, 1904.

Stockton, Lewis. *Marriage, Civil and Ecclesiastical.* privately printed. Buffalo, 1912.

Stone, Lawrence. *The Family, Sex, and Marriage in England 1500–1800.* New York: Harper & Row, 1977.

Taylor, G. Ratray. *Sex in History.* London: Thames & Hudson, 1953.

Tickner, F. W. *Women in English Economic History.* London: Dent, 1923.

Tilly, L. A., J. W. Scott, and M. Cohen, "Women's Work and the European Fertility Pattern." *Journal of Interdisciplinary History,* VI, No. 3(Winter 1976), pp. 447–476.

Troyer, Howard William. *Ned Ward of Grub Street*. Cambridge, Mass.: Harvard University Press, 1946.

Watt, Ian. *The Rise of the Novel*. Berkeley: University of California Press, 1957.

Whicher, George Frisbie. *The Life and Romances of Eliza Haywood*. New York: Columbia University Press, 1915.

Wiles, R. M. "Middle-Class Literacy in Eighteenth Century England: Fresh Evidence," in *Studies in the Eighteenth Century*. ed. R. F. Brissenden. Canberra: Australian National University Press, 1968, pp. 49–66.

Woolf, Virginia. *The Second Common Reader*. New York: Harcourt, Brace, and Company, 1932.

Wright, Louis B. *Middle-Class Culture in Elizabethan England*. Chapel Hill: University of North Carolina Press, 1935.

Würzbach, Natascha, ed. *The Novel in Letters: Epistolary Fiction in the Early English Novel, 1678–1740*. Coral Gables, Florida: University of Miami Press, 1969.

Index